THAMES PATHWAY

Journal of a walk along the Thames Pathway

Keith Pauling

First published 2009

All rights reserved

Copyright Keith Pauling 2009

ISBN 978-1-4452-2239-4

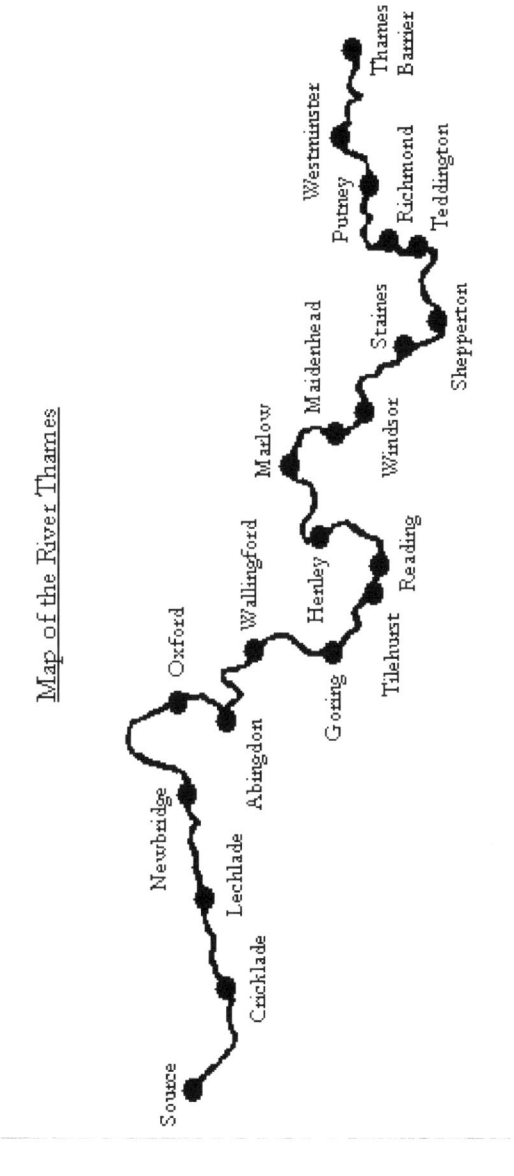

INTRODUCTION

Sometimes there is the urge to do something different. But do what; exactly? This is what hit me in the late autumn of 2007.

As John Lennon once famously said, "Life is what happens while you are making plans".

This fit, feisty, rebellious teenager that was going to change the world had been through the standard phases of life; marriage, kids, mortgage, climbing and slipping on the greasy-pole of career ambition and what was the result? I had gone from fit to fat. Long-haired and young had become hair long-gone. In the football match of life I was playing out a steady 1-1 draw with the clock running mid-way through the second half and desperately hoping that the manager was not going to sub me off before the final whistle.

The human brain is a wonderful thing. We cram it with all sorts of random bits and bobs and provided we leave it to its own devices it is capable of coming up with the most amazing solutions. My own grey-matter absorbed all of my life history to date, and came up with its proposal.

Walk along the Thames and write about it.

There is only one option to take in these situations. In the words of the Nike advert – "Just Do It".

I set off on Saturday April 26th 2008 from the source near Kemble, and finished at the Thames Flood Barrier twelve days later. This is my journal of the walk, the scenery, the fascinating places and remarkable histories surrounding the River Thames.

The walk was sponsored by friends and family in aid of The British Heart Foundation.

Cover Photographs

Upper;   River Thames at Hurley

Lower;   Reflections at Newbridge

DAY ONE

SOURCE TO CRICKLADE

12.3 Miles

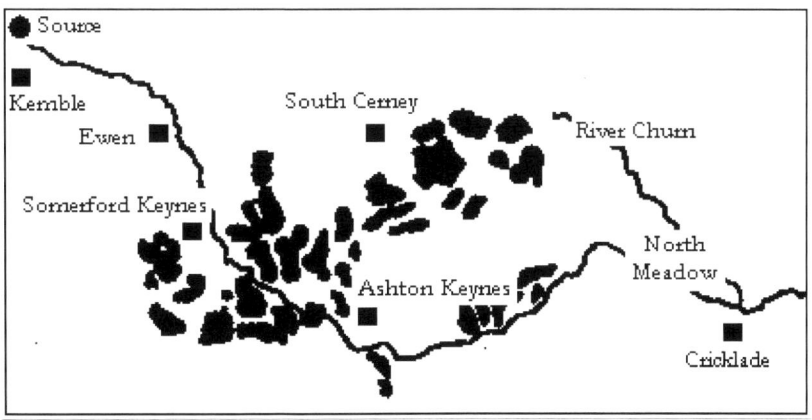

The Source

The official source of the Thames lies in a remote Gloucestershire meadow on the edge of the small village of Kemble. Ordnance Survey map reference ST980994 to be absolutely precise. This area is officially known as Trewsbury Mead but is sometimes referred to as Thames Head.

One hundred and eighty four miles of the River Thames stretch out between here and the Flood Barrier at Greenwich. It is a daunting thought. Looking on the bright side I am standing here at a height of 361 feet above sea level so in theory it should be all downhill from here.

Below the branches of an old ash tree stands the source marker stone which bears the following inscription;

The Conservation of the River Thames
1857 – 1974
This stone was placed here to mark the
Source of the River Thames

Up until 1974 the statue of "Old Father Thames" himself would have welcomed visitors to the source. He has since been moved to a more accessible location at St. John's Lock and I will be making his acquaintance in two days time.

Not everyone is in absolute agreement that this is the true source of the Thames. The Ordnance Survey and the Environment Agency both give Trewsbury Mead as the official source, but there is a small rival faction that argues that the source is at Seven Springs, approximately eleven miles to the north of where I am standing. A look at the map reveals that Seven Springs is marked as the source of the River Churn which is only regarded as a tributary of the Thames and joins with the main river just below Cricklade. Both rivers have had their names since earliest recorded history and there seems little cause for the argument. The Churn has given its name to the villages of North and South Cerney, and also to the town of Cirencester which was known to the Romans as Corinium. Just as some people will continue to argue that the world is flat so they will dispute the source of the Thames from time to time.

All that be as it may, but the map says that the source is here, the stone is here, and I am here. The only snag is that there is just no sign of any water here.

Despite the recent rains the first part of my journey is along a dry depression in the field. The headwater springs can apparently come instantly to life after particularly heavy rainfall and at such times this bowl has been known to flood very quickly. There are tales that in Victorian times one only had to jab a stick into the ground anywhere in this field to be rewarded by the release of a spurt of spring-water.

Within a few hundred yards the shallow depression noticeably transforms into a dry river bed, but it takes almost 10 minutes of walking before a puddle appears. This is it, the first water of the Thames. Away I go!

Only a few yards later I am following what I can only describe as a shallow reed-filled ditch, but in the space of only a few minutes this undergoes a rapid metamorphosis into a sparkly clear stream running under a simple stone footbridge. This is the first of many bridges ending with the distinctive shape of Tower Bridge that will provide me with handy marker points along the pathway. Shortly afterwards the first road bridge appears and sweeps the fledgling waterway under the lane and across the fields on its journey to the sea.

I follow the river with a bright spring in my step, enjoying the first stage of my expedition. It is a delightful spring morning and the weather forecast for this weekend is ideal. Sunshine with a light breeze to cool me from my exertions will make this an ideal opening day. The people at the Met Office are not so optimistic for the remainder of the week and are predicting persistent rainfall from Tuesday.

The first village I come to on the river is named Ewen, which means "source of a river". I have been walking for some while now, but the subject of my mission is merely a small infant stream carrying only a few inches of water and is still not much more than a ditch. At Ewen I discover the first water-mill on the river. It seems incredible to think that a mill could operate with such a tiny water flow, but years ago before the water-table fell to its present level operate it surely did.

In many places the river is so small that it could be jumped over with ease if I so wished. However, as field after field goes by wider pools appear and the depths are increasing. Butterflies and insect life abound and a peaceful air prevails. A swan's nest complete with a pair of mute swans is half hidden among the reeds on the opposite bank. The sun reflects off newly formed leaves and the occasional patch of early yellow rapeseed adds a variety to the distant greenery. The English countryside is in its full glory.

Cotswold Water Park

I cross a wooden footbridge and suddenly there is a dramatic change in the landscape. Without warning there are lakes, and there are lots of them.

I have arrived at Neigh Bridge Country Park which is just one of over 140 lakes that make up the Cotswold Water Park. The total area covered by the water park is around 40 square miles and the guide book claims that this complex is the largest inland man-made water feature in Europe.

The natural grassy pathway has been transformed into a gravel and pebble surface that winds its way between the lakes. A whole new environment is opening up around me.

I am a little surprised by the number of people that are here going about their various leisure pursuits. There are bird watchers, anglers, cyclists, boaters as well as plenty of other walkers all enjoying the tranquil lakes in their own preferential way.

So how come all of these lakes are here in the first place? To answer that question we have to go back millions of years to the time of the formation of the Cotswold Hills. Since their formation, the hills have been steadily eroded away by the elements and the sands and gravel were deposited here in this area of North Wiltshire. These deposits typically start at around one metre below the surface and the depths of the seams can be from just a few centimetres to more than six metres.

The sands and gravels have a high value in the construction industry and the mineral companies soon moved in. When the sand and gravel are removed it leaves behind a hole in the ground. With the relatively high water table in this area any hole of more than a metre depth rapidly fills with water, and "hey-presto" there is another lake!

Currently there are seven different mineral companies extracting two million tonnes of gravel per year. Fifty years of extraction has seen the creation of 147 lakes, and there is still an estimated 50 years of useful mineral resource remaining to be removed from the ground.

Cotswold Water Park was first designated in 1967 in order to make a better recreational and environmental use of what were then relatively ugly water-filled gravel workings. These former unsightly workings are being converted into a spectacular giant leisure park and nature reserve.

The first lakes were simple rectangular pits with steep, straight sides. This may have been simpler for extracting gravel, but for restoring the land afterwards it was totally useless. Improved restoration planning and design created inlets, islands and shallows that made the environment much healthier for both fish and wildlife. The region has literally blossomed ever since.

What a marvelous range of wildlife there is to be seen in this water-filled world. The bird spotters are out in force today, keenly observing the warblers and chiff chaffs. Shortly these birds will be joined by incoming willow warblers, sedge warblers and black caps. If I am very lucky I may catch a fleeting glimpse of one of the many kingfishers that have made the water park their home, but knowing how the fates play their games with me I will probably have to settle for being hissed at by a flock of Canada Geese.

The first dragonflies and butterflies are darting around in the air, and very soon the first of the orchids will open up their flowers. There are allegedly twenty three different species of dragonfly that can be found in the area including the relatively rare downy emerald dragonfly.

The abundant population of insects attracts their own predators, and consequently there are large numbers of bats that find this a veritable smorgasbord of delight. Believe it or not there are fourteen different species of bat that have made the water park their home.

On Flagham Fen a more adventurous wildlife project is underway. The lake is surrounded by an electrified fence which at first seems a little over the top to keep the stray walker out. A quick read of the many information boards around the perimeter soon reveals that it is not to keep people out; it is to keep its inhabitants in! European Beavers have been introduced as an experiment, and by all accounts they seem to be settling in nicely. The theory runs that these creatures will improve the ecology of the lake with their foraging and living habits allowing the plant-life to flourish without too much additional help from man. It will be wonderful if it is a success and these beautiful creatures can be integrated into this environment.

The park is easily accessed by the public by over 150km of paths, bridleways and cycle-ways. Dotted among the lakes are fourteen picturesque villages with over 20,000 inhabitants.

I thought I had travelled all over our islands but this was all new to me. How could there be more than 40 square miles of lakes of which I had previously been unaware? Come on then, admit it; were you aware that this water-filled area existed before reading it here?

There is plenty of space to get away from it all before everyone else finds out about Cotswold Water Park. The park is not only a superb place for walkers and cyclists but also an excellent peaceful retreat for families to relax by the many lakesides. Family games of tennis and cricket were under way, frisbees span through the air and the occasional colourful kite could be seen in the sky.

Ashton Keynes is the largest village in the area. It takes its name from the de Kaines family who arrived with William the Conqueror and stayed with us, taking over these local lands from the resident Saxons.

The great chronicler of England, William Cobbett, described Ashton Keynes as "a very curious place" when he passed through in 1826. The river here divides into several channels, each squeezing its way through different parts of the village before joining up again to continue on its way. Many of the streams run parallel with pathways, and small stone bridges have been built across the streams to give access to properties, making a sort of rural miniature version of Venice. Delightful well-maintained cottage gardens add their colour and it seems that everywhere I turn there is another "chocolate box" scene to attract the eye.

As I come to the main road through the village I discover an old stone "Preaching Cross". The village boasts a total of four such crosses. Quite why such a small place possesses as many as four of them is a mystery that I did not find an answer to in my researches. It is, however, no surprise that after finding four crosses in such close proximity to discover that the village church is very appropriately named "Holy Cross". A previous generation showed their imagination by converting the cross situated in the churchyard to its current use as the village war memorial.

All of the crosses were damaged during the Civil War by the Roundheads, who I discovered were responsible for quite a lot of the vandalism to our heritage in this part of the country. "The Roundheads are coming" must have spread the same fears in the local community in the seventeenth century as would happen today if the village football club suddenly found themselves drawn at home to Millwall in the FA Cup.

The pathway turns left at the road junction, but I ignore the demands of the way-marker and instead turn right to seek out the White Hart, which is just a little way along the road. Another one of the preaching crosses stands proudly outside the pub. Inside there are original paintings decorating the walls and the general ambience provides a bright and cheery welcome for the weary walker.

Fortified by a couple of pints and a crispy bacon baguette I return to the pathway and follow it as it threads through the village, first following a lane and then cutting across the playing fields. Soon I am back among the lakes. An area to my left is fenced off and displays the stern warning

"Dangerous Quicksand". The vengeful thought passed through my mind that it would have restored some justice if these quicksands had previously managed to trap the vandalising Roundheads in revenge for the damaged crosses as they made their route out of the village.

The peace is broken by a distant hum, which slowly increases in volume as I walk along. The sound reaches a full roar and I turn a corner to discover a new lake before me. The noise is caused by a water-skier who is in sole possession of the lake. One of the huge advantages this complex has is its ability to allocate specific territories to those whose recreation is not fully compatible with that of others. One can appreciate that this particular enthusiast would not endear himself to yachtsmen as they sail around, and most certainly would unsettle the bird population and their attendant twitchers. Here the skier can blast across the water on his own allocated lake without the risk of upsetting other users. I decide to sit and watch for a while, but the skier seems pretty well in control and a dramatic plunge into the water just for my entertainment seems unlikely, so I move on.

All of the time since I left Ashton Keynes the Thames has worked its own way through the gravel pits while I have followed the paths through the complex, but now we are re-acquainted and travel together towards Cricklade. The tower of the Parish Church of St Sampson's becomes visible in the distance, creating a destination marker for the end of day one.

Before I reach the town there is the botanical highlight of the day.

North Meadow

Most of the first day's walking has been through man-made landscape. After the source and the early headstream of the infant river had been left behind the hand (or more accurately for the water park the JCB) of man has been responsible for shaping my surroundings. Now it is time to restore the balance with a dramatic return to natural land use. I have arrived at one of the finest tracts of uncultivated meadowland that we have left in these islands, the tranquil and unspoilt North Meadow.

The use of the land of North Meadow has been carefully regulated throughout the ages under the strict control of the local official known as the "Hayward". In olden days the hay cutting would begin on July 1st, and cattle were not allowed to graze on it until Lammas Day, which falls on August 1st. Horses were then permitted to run free on the meadow from September, and sheep were allowed to join the party shortly afterwards until winter set in. On Candlemass Eve (February 12th) it was a case of "everybody off" in order to let the hay grow again. Several ancient carved stones still stand on the meadow to mark the boundary positions of the old hay lots.

Many centuries of the constant cycle of hay cutting and grazing interspersed with occasional flooding have made this place into a botanists dream. Occupying 110 acres between the River Thames and the River Churn the meadow is filled with colourful flowers. Plants found here include adder's tongue, great burnet, marsh marigold, water crowfoot, buttercup and celandine. However, the flower that this haven is most noted for is the one that many visitors come here at this time of year specifically to admire. Flowering in late spring, this is the home of the Snake's Head Fritillary.

Fritillaria Meleagris to give its full Latin name is one of our rarest flowers. The name is derived from the Latin *fritillus* which translates as "dice box". This alludes to the chequered pattern seen on the flower.

Approximately 80% of all of the wild plants of this species found in Britain live in North Meadow. The plant can also be found in smaller numbers at Ducklington near Witney, which has its own Fritillary Festival to celebrate the flower. Later on during the walk I will pass Magdalene College Field in the city of Oxford which is where most of the remainder are to be found.

The plant varies between 15cm and 40cm in height and has a nodding bell-shaped flower of around 2cm in diameter. The Snake's Head variety has a chequered reddish-brown purple appearance, but occasionally also appears in white.

At one time the fritillaries were picked and sent to Covent Garden, but now they are considered to be an endangered species in the wild and as such are vigorously protected. Cultivation of meadowland has been responsible for their demise in all but the three places in England, but here on North Meadow they happily flower and proliferate. From a distance the meadow appears to possess a purple tinted haze, but as I approach and can see the finer detail the haze is the effect of literally millions of the small purple flowers. The purple colouring is interspersed with the occasional white specimen, and there are some additional bright yellow dots caused by the presence of dandelions.

A quick something here for any quiz buffs. The fritillary is the official flower of the Swedish Province of Uppsala and also appears on the national symbol of Croatia. As the man said, "Not a lot of people know that". If you win a pub quiz because of that good luck to you. (And a pint for too me please).

The area fair buzzes with insect life. Butterflies and damselflies are seemingly everywhere, and the river, which is still no more than a stream, attracts reed bunting and sedge warblers along with some stately-looking swans who patrol the waters with an arrogance that makes it appear that they think they own the place, and not (as we shall see later on the walk) the other way around.

Cricklade

Guided by the tower of St Sampson's Church I have arrived at Cricklade. The name means "place of the river crossing". The town lies just off the old Roman road that was known as Ermin Street which connected the old towns of Newbury and Gloucester. The ground hereabouts in those days was nearly all wetland and could only be crossed with great difficulty. Roman engineers built a raised causeway to cross the marshes, and a settlement was formed on the south bank of the crossing.

The settlement continued to grow after the departure of the Romans. It became a Saxon "New Town", so in its own way it is much like an earlier version of Milton Keynes only without the roundabouts. Cricklade became a full Saxon Borough in 887.

King Alfred formed a garrison here to protect Wessex against marauders, so greatly increasing the local population. Records show that up to 1500 men were stationed at Cricklade to protect the Wessex homeland.

An indication of the importance that Cricklade held in those far-off days was that the town possessed its own mint. Coins were struck here from 979 until 1100 and some of the coins can still be seen today by visitors to the local museums.

In 1821 William Cobbett visited during his travels and described Cricklade as "a villainous place". Quite how he could have described this peaceful and quiet town in such terms is a mystery. A tranquil air is much in evidence even on this relatively busy Saturday afternoon as people go about their weekend.

For some distance from Cricklade the only sign that a town may exist at all was the sight of St Sampson's tower. This cathedral-like tower was added to the church by the Duke of Northumberland (who was the Father-in-Law of Lady Jane Grey), in 1553. Inside the tower one can find, somewhat surprisingly, the heart, club, diamond and spade of a pack of playing cards. This has caused some historians to form the opinion that the building of the tower was financed from the proceeds of a successful gamble.

I take a short diversion from the marked path to take a look at the rather splendid "Jubilee Clock" that stands by the road junction at the top of the High Street. The white-faced clock sits in a striking red cube supported by a black column adorned with a white spiral decoration. It was put here to commemorate the Diamond Jubilee of Queen Victoria in 1897

A little further along the street I come to the much restored early Norman St Mary's church. This is considerably older than St Sampson's, and in 1983 was re-consecrated to a Roman Catholic Church, making it officially the oldest church used for Catholic worship in England. A fine 14th Century preaching cross stands in the churchyard.

The Town Bridge marks the official start of navigation on the River Thames. (Or the end if you are travelling upstream). It may not look it now, but up until 1830 there was a thriving wharf here that was believed to have existed since Roman times. Whilst this is the official limit of navigation, the impracticality of moving any boat through these waters is obvious even to me, because the river passing under the Town Bridge is still little more than a brook.

I have reached the end of my journey for day one. The next stage of the walk will take me on to Lechlade, the highest practical point for navigation on the Thames. Between here and there the waters will be swollen by a succession of tributaries, and it will be a very different river by this time tomorrow.

DAY TWO

CRICKLADE TO LECHLADE

10.9 Miles

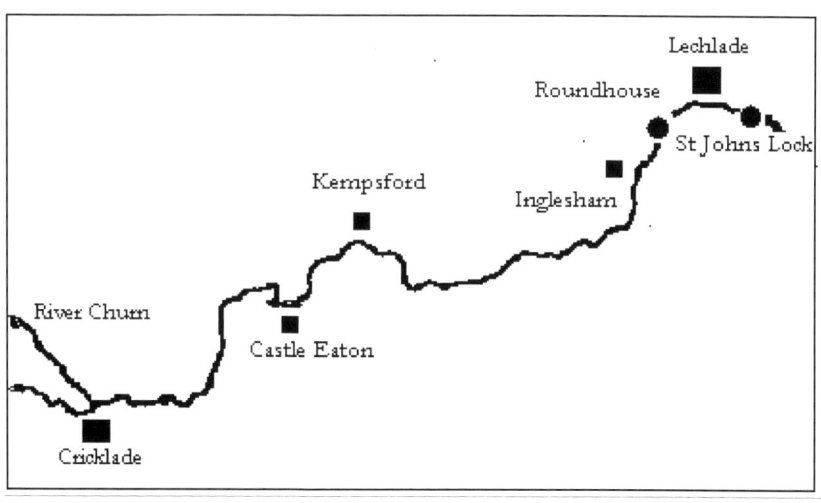

Cricklade to Kempsford

The addition of the waters of the River Churn to the Thames below Cricklade suddenly increases both the depth and the width of the river. This increases again shortly afterwards with two more tributaries, the River Key and the River Ray making their contributions to the expanding flow. Within a short walk of Cricklade the river and its associated surroundings move up the scale by a few notches. Footbridges become taller and longer, and it would be a foolhardy walker who now tried to leap between the banks as was possible for most of the previous day.

The pathway follows a succession of footbridges that cross over the many water channels that discharge their flows into the main river. I pass through water-meadow after water-meadow and cross bridge after bridge as the river widens and deepens over the next four miles.

Without warning the track suddenly veers away from the river towards the village of Castle Eaton. As I approach the village I look in vain among the rows of stone cottages for the castle, but I am assured that there isn't one.

The path leaves the riverside for a while and uses narrow lanes before rejoining the river near Kempsford. This is one of those places that defy all logic when you look at its history. Here we are in Wiltshire, and yet in medieval times the village was a part of the Duchy of Lancaster. Even with the technology we have at our disposal today for anyone to attempt to administer a village from almost the other end of the country would prove to be what the management gurus like to term "challenging". So how did they do it in the 14th century with none of the communication services we take for granted these days? Mind you, the messenger service in those days was probably still quicker than the post office is today, so perhaps they had some advantages after all.

Kempsford gained by its association with Lancaster when John of Gaunt arranged for the building of a new church tower. He commissioned the construction of the tower to be a memorial to his late wife, and it was completed in 1390. Again, imagine for a moment the difficulty that this must have involved in those days. Anyone who has had the builders in can relate many tales of frustration with their timekeeping and progress of the job. How did John of Gaunt "keep an eye" on the builders from his northern homeland?

After a short meeting with the river, the pathway separates again and follows a wide bridle path to Inglesham. The river is mostly hidden from my sight during this part of the walk, but reassuringly still lays only a couple of fields away to my left, taking its own lonely route in parallel to the pathway.

This is the longest section that I will experience on the entire walk where the pathway does not run alongside the riverbank. The bridleway is a pleasant enough walk, but I stride purposely onwards towards Inglesham, where I will rejoin the river to travel together once more.

Inglesham

Inglesham is the most northern outpost of Wiltshire, snuggled up against the borders with Gloucestershire and Oxfordshire. Some doubt that is should be in Wiltshire at all, but the powers that be insist that it lies within the unitary authority of Swindon and so it is definitely situated in Wiltshire. Quite what the locals think of their lovely little hamlet being considered a part of dreary Swindon I did not discover.

The map shows Inglesham to be a "lost medieval village (site of)". All that remains now is a couple of farms, a handful of cottages and a very interesting church.

The church of St John the Baptist was restored in the 19th century in the style of its original 13th century origins. This was due to the determination and campaigning of William Morris who lived at the nearby Kelmscott Manor. (We will look at the life of William Morris in more detail a little later).

It was common at that time for restorations to be carried out in the contemporary Victorian Gothic style, but Morris was adamant that this particular building should be placed firmly back in the 13th century from where it originated. After much vigorous campaigning Morris won everyone over to his view, and the restoration work was carried out accordingly. So here we have a fine building with 13th century stonework on the outside, and decorated with wall paintings and texts dating from the same period on the inside. The church also features a Jacobean pulpit and old-style box pews, including one originally reserved for his own private use by the local squire of the manor.

The building today is well looked after and maintained by the Churches Conservation Trust and is open to the public on most days.

The Roundhouse and the Thames and Severn Canal

The river is now back in full view, and a short walk across the field returns me to the riverbank at the Roundhouse.

The Round House marks the upper end of navigation on the Thames. To the right of the building is the entrance to the Thames and Severn Canal. This canal linked the Thames to the Stroudwater Navigation at

Wallbridge, near Stroud, and thence to the Gloucester Canal and River Severn.

Work started in 1783 and the canal was opened in 1789 at a total cost of £250,000. The chief engineer for the project was Josiah Clowes, who earned himself a formidable reputation for his work. He was paid a salary of £300 which was an enormous amount of money for a civil engineer in those days. He was highly sought after for other civil engineering projects during his lifetime, and oversaw many other canal projects including the Dudley Tunnel.

The canal was just a little less than 29 miles long, and used 44 locks to cope with the changes in the geography. The highest point of the canal was the Sapperton Tunnel at 363 feet above sea level. At the time of its construction this tunnel was the longest in England, measuring 2.1 miles.

All of Josiah Clowes ingenuity in the construction of the canal could not defeat a major flaw with the design. Natural springs kept breaking through the clay lining of the canal bed in the higher stretches. In the summer the springs would recede, and the holes remaining would drain the water at a faster rate than could be replenished and the canal would start to run dry. Various remedies were tried, including reducing the sides of the locks and relining one section with concrete.

The final demise was caused by economic competition. The arrival of the railways captured most of the commercial traffic, and the canal started to struggle through the late 1800s. By 1927 the situation had become absolute and the canal was mostly abandoned, although some traffic still used the western stretches until 1933. The canal is currently undergoing an intensive restoration programme managed by the Stroudwater and Severn Canal Trust.

The Roundhouse marks the start of the navigable River Thames. There is an immediate advantage to the walker in that there is now an official maintained towpath alongside the Thames from this point that will be my companion for a good many miles downstream to Putney.

Boats are moored up everywhere, and from this moment onwards barges and cruisers will be a very common sight along the waterway.

The river bank here is extremely popular for riverside walkers and family picnics. The weather has brightened into a sunny afternoon which has brought the crowds out onto the meadows. The riverside pub looks particularly busy, and it looks such a nice place to sit for a while, and I have made good time, and……..

Lechlade

It is a short distance to Halfpenny Bridge which could be considered the first "proper" bridge of the river in that it has sufficient headroom to allow river-craft to pass freely underneath. There are 106 more bridges that cross the navigable river between Lechlade and the Flood Barrier. Halfpenny Bridge was constructed in 1792 by James Hollingsworth, and the clearance of 4.72M (15ft 6in) was high enough at that time to avoid the need to lower the masts of the vessels passing beneath.

It does not stretch the imagination much to discover that the bridge originally took its name from the toll originally levied for crossing it. It was not a popular toll (are they ever?) and the locals were having none of it. Resentment increased every year and in 1839 they rebelled and all banded together and refused to pay the toll. This inevitably led to some lively altercations with the toll collectors, and people tended to cross the bridge in groups in a show of strength to make it easier for them to resist the demands of the toll gatherers. All efforts at extracting tolls were finally abandoned in 1875 and the bridge has been toll-free ever since. Perhaps some of the descendants of those early liberators would like to accompany me down to London and campaign to get rid of Cuddly Ken's much hated London congestion charge. (NB In a few days time and before I reach the capital, Cuddly Ken was displaced by Bouncing Boris, but the detested congestion "toll" still remained in place).

Lechlade is mentioned in the Doomsday Book, and has been a major borough since the early 12th century. The town signs announce that Lechlade is an inland port, and this was the foundation of its wealth. Although the town was a major force for the English wool trade, Lechlade's primary function was as a staging post for freight to London. Cotswold wool and the finest Gloucestershire cheeses were the main goods that were brought to the wharves of Lechlade for transfer to the river barges that would take them to the commercial market places of London. The opening of the Severn and Thames Canal increased the volume of trade immensely and the town grew very wealthy as a consequence.

The landmark church dates from 1476 and is considered to be one of the finest in Gloucestershire. It is believed that it was dedicated to St Lawrence at the wish of Catherine of Aragon whose pomegranate symbol can be seen on the vestry door.

The poet Percy Bysshe Shelley visited Lechlade in September 1815. Standing in the churchyard with Mary his wife, and friends Charles Claremont and Thomas Love Peacock he watched the sun setting and was inspired to write his poem "Summer Evening Churchyard, Lechlade".

THE wind has swept from the wide atmosphere
Each vapour that obscured the sunset's ray,
And pallid Evening twines its beaming hair
In duskier braids around the languid eyes of Day:
Silence and Twilight, unbeloved of men,
Creep hand in hand from yon obscurest glen.

They breathe their spells towards the departing day,
Encompassing the earth, air, stars, and sea;
Light, sound, and motion, own the potent sway,
Responding to the charm with its own mystery.
The winds are still, or the dry church-tower grass
Knows not their gentle motions as they pass.

Thou too, aerial pile, whose pinnacles
Point from one shrine like pyramids of fire,
Obey'st in silence their sweet solemn spells,
Clothing in hues of heaven thy dim and distant spire,
Around whose lessening and invisible height
Gather among the stars the clouds of night.

The dead are sleeping in their sepulchres:
And, mouldering as they sleep, a thrilling sound,
Half sense half thought, among the darkness stirs,
Breathed from their wormy beds all living things around,
And, mingling with the still night and mute sky,
Its awful hush is felt inaudibly.

Thus solemnized and softened, death is mild
And terrorless as this serenest night.
Here could I hope, like some enquiring child
Sporting on graves, that death did hide from human sight
Sweet secrets, or beside its breathless sleep
That loveliest dreams perpetual watch did keep.

St John's Lock and Father Thames

Leaving the buildings of Lechlade behind, it is a short walk across a couple of fields to the first of the 46 locks of the Thames.

St John's Lock derives its name from a priory that was established here in 1250, which unfortunately no longer exists.

The requirement for a lock here came from the opening of the Thames and Severn canal that I passed a short while ago. It was necessary to maintain a navigable depth of water from the end of the canal once vessels had moved on to the main river. The original pound lock was constructed of stone by J.Knock in 1790.

The first lock house was built in 1830. Previously to that date the lock keeper had always resided at the nearby Trout Inn, but the Thames Navigation Commission brought in a rule that prohibited publicans from being lock keepers, and so he had to move. I wonder how this would play with 21st century employment legislation. Anyway, the lock keeper may well still have spent all his time in the hostelry because the lock fell into a poor state of repair and had to be restored in 1867. Further deterioration followed and the lock was replaced in 1905.

I have reached a significant marker on my journey, for upon reaching St. John's Lock it is time for me to pay my respects to Old Father

Thames. The old boy reclines by the side of the lock, keeping a watchful eye on the boats as they pass through.

The statue was commissioned to stand by the fountains in the grounds of Crystal Palace for the Great Exhibition of 1851. It was sculpted from a solid block of Portland stone by Rafaelle Monti, a renowned Italian sculptor of his day. Monti was born in 1818 and studied his art in Vienna and Milan before coming to England in 1848. His exhibitions at the Royal Academy soon made him much in demand and many fine works were crafted by him until his death in 1881.

Old Father Thames spent his early years at Crystal Palace, and was fortunate to survive the fire that destroyed it in 1936. The Thames Conservancy purchased him in 1958 and sited him at Trewsbury Mead where the pathway begins. There he stood in loneliness with just a few sheep and an occasional walker with whom to pass the time. He must have been relieved when in 1974 he was moved to his current location at the first lock on the river.

I can only imagine that he must be much happier here than at his former location at the source. Here he can be content as he is surrounded by the bustling activity of the lock as boaters, walkers and those simply passing the time all enjoy his river.

DAY THREE

LECHLADE TO NEWBRIDGE

16.4 Miles

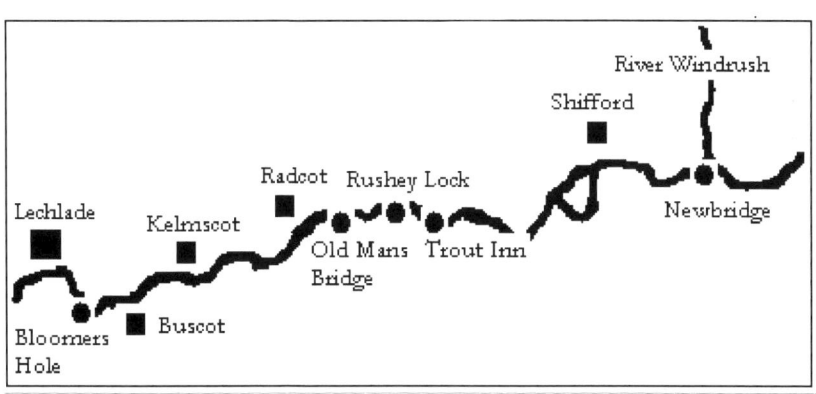

Bloomers Hole

Immediately below St Johns Bridge the river receives two injections of water to feed the growing river. The River Cole and River Leach add their contributions from opposite banks and the combined waters continue their journey downstream.

Shortly afterwards I cross the Thames by the newest bridge across the river at Bloomers Hole. The bridge was specifically commissioned by the Countryside Agency to complete the Thames Pathway. It was constructed by Oxfordshire County Council under the direction of Charlie Benner, the senior engineer.

The bridge at first appears to be made of wood, but appearances as is so often the case can be deceptive. The wood is only the cladding, with the real hard work being carried out by two 27 foot-long steel spans, each weighing eight tonnes. The whole construction was pre-assembled and airlifted into place by a Chinook helicopter from nearby RAF Brize Norton.

Exactly how this stretch of river came to bear the name of Bloomer's Hole is something of a mystery. There is Bloomers Hole and also Bloomers Meadow, but who exactly was Bloomer? Two stories have emerged, neither of which have any great provenance. The first is that a carter by the name of Bloomer was drowned below these waters while attempting to cross the river at this point with his wagon and horse. A sad tale if it is true. More entertainment can be gathered from the second story by standing on the new bridge and imagining the local Rector, the Reverend Bloomer, delightfully splashing about in the refreshing waters below while enjoying his favourite past-time of skinny-dipping. His "au naturelle" aquatic activities allegedly shocked his more staid parishioners into a state of apoplexy. It reminds me of the old favourite;

Parish Lady; "It is disgusting, I could see everything."

Rev Bloomer; "Madam, I don't think you can see anything at all from the village".

Parish Lady; "I can if I climb to the top of the apple tree by the blacksmiths".

Meanders and Pill Boxes

I am now entering the Thames at its most tranquil. For the next 30 miles the river meanders its way to Oxford through lonely water-meadows with only the occasional glimpse of distant farms and villages. Here I became as one with my surroundings. Only the sounds of nature disturb the air. Birds sing, the river ripples on its course, and the insects and butterflies go about their daily business.

The path is extremely well maintained. The fencing keeps the traveler to the riverbank but it does not seem to intrude upon the pathway, keeping its distance from the waters edge while maintaining its major function of guarding the farmers land.

The river meanders its way downstream, with twists and turns so severe in places that it seems that it sometimes wants to join up with itself. Meanders derive their name from a river of that name in Asia Minor that featured very pronounced bends and loops. The name of the river was adopted to describe any stretch of water that exhibited such features.

An interesting snippet of information that I came across while conducting my research is that if you take the straight line distance between the source of a river and its mouth, multiply by PI (3.142), it will be found to be approximately the full length of the river as it flows. This may sound incredible although along this section of the Thames it seemed something of an understatement.

Gradually the realisation dawns on me that following the riverbank is probably adding several miles to the journey. How much shorter would the route be if water not only always flowed downhill, but also always flowed in straight lines?

These thoughts were replaced with an exciting game of "where will the river go next?" Will it be towards the trees on the left or the bushes on the right? As I progressed the way forward was slowly uncovered but only by a little at a time. It was as if the waters wanted to retain their mysteries and only reveal the next enticing secret in their own time.

After a while I begin to notice the regular appearance of concrete "pill boxes" along the north bank of the river. Some were so eroded that they looked like tiny grey castles. What were they doing so far away from any obvious strategic military target?

The boxes are here because during World War II this was designated as "Stopline Red". If we were invaded this is where the enemy would be brought to a juddering halt before they could reach the Midlands.

At this point some logical thinking started to set in. Which bright-spark in the War Office decided that the might of the German High Command would ignore all of the major roads and bridges and take their heavy Panzer divisions across the remote water-meadows of West Oxfordshire? And how, exactly, were these boxes in which you could not fit more than a handful of men, expected to bring about this sudden halt to Adolf's cunning plan? Did they expect that having come this far that Jerry would see the pill box filled with the local Captain Mainwaring and his Dads Army finest, shout "Gott in Himmel ! Ve vill never vin !", and turn back to get home in time for the Oktoberfest?

It was our good fortune that this defensive shield was never required to be put to the ultimate test. So here the boxes stand in their own silent tribute to those uncertain times, while the elements slowly erode their walls and mother-nature works her magic to re-establish her dominance over their intrusion. In some unfathomable way the concrete abhorrations contribute something to the atmosphere, adding a certain serenity of their own. We will leave them to stand for as long as they may.

Buscot Lock

I follow the meanders of the river and arrive at Buscot Lock, which holds the distinction of being the smallest of the 45 Thames locks at only 33.47M in length. The lock was built at the same time as St Johns Lock, by the same engineer J.Nock. The weir was rebuilt in 1979 and this has created a lovely weir pool that is now overlooked by a popular National Trust picnic area.

The area around Buscot was revolutionised by a certain Mr. Robert Tertius Campbell during the 19th Century.

In 1859 Campbell returned to England from Australia, where he had made his fortune in the goldfields. He bought the semi-derelict Buscot Park Estate, which at that time was mostly pastureland, and set about converting it into one of the most industrialised farms of the Victorian era.

The first stage of the project was to drain the existing farmland. He then constructed a twenty-acre reservoir, and fed it by installing two pumps driven by the weirs at Buscot and Eaton Hastings. The final part of the conversion was to use the reservoir to irrigate the whole 3,500 acres of the estate by cutting drainage channels into the fields. The work was carried out under the direction of Baldwin Latham, a noted civil engineer.

The general workings of the estate were well ahead of its time. Cultivation of the land was by giant Fowler ploughing engines, which were twice the size of engines commonly used elsewhere. They pulled six-furrow ploughs, and on many occasions worked though the night in order to prepare the fields for cultivation.

The estate had its own gasworks, and its own plants for the production of oil cake, fertiliser and vitriol. With what we have learned about Campbell's efficient practices it is no surprise to learn that the raw materials for the fertiliser and vitriol were recycled by-products from the gas-works and the estate.

All of this required a high level of management and communication. In order to make this as speedy and efficient as possible Campbell introduced a telegraph system that covered the entire estate so that his managers were always able to pass instructions and keep up with developments wherever they were situated

Campbell also introduced some other practices which are still controversial today. He used accelerated fattening methods with sugar beet feeds, and kept cattle in what we would term "battery" conditions. On the other hand he had a reputation as a good employer, and introduced a maximum nine-hour day for his labourers, which was virtually unheard of in those days.

It was Campbell's wildest scheme that was to lead to his eventual undoing. In a venture that would have Duncan Bannatyne screaming "Aahm Oot!" within seconds, our dear Robert set up a distillery to make spirit alcohol from his sugar beet and export it to France.

The distillery was situated just above Buscot Lock and opened in 1869. In a similar vein to Campbell's other initiatives it was a model of industrial efficiency. To collect the beet from the farms around the estate he built a narrow-gauge railway with over six miles of track. The railway used three steam locomotives that were named after Campbell's three daughters, Edith, Emily and Alice.

Campbell continuously claimed that the estate and the factories made a profit, but by the mid 1870's many were questioning whether he was covering his enormous investment costs. He had taken out huge mortgages to pay for all of the development work. Demand for his exported alcohol trade was being crushed by the Franco-Prussian War, and he had attracted the unwanted attention of the gentlemen from Customs and Excise. All of this started to seriously affect his health, and in 1879, only ten years after it opened, the distillery, the factories and all of their assets were sold off for whatever the Estate could realise in an attempt to cut the rapidly accumulating losses.

The remarkable enterprise had come to an end after only twenty years. However, many of the estate facilities were to function for many years afterwards, and parts of the irrigation scheme are still in use today.

Robert Tertius Campbell must have been a fascinating and inventive character with ideas well ahead of his time.

The estate was purchased by a very successful city financier, Alexander Henderson who later became the first Lord Faringdon, and his descendants continue to live here today.

The House is home to the Faringdon Collection which contains many paintings and objets d'art. British art of the 19th and 20th centuries are particularly well represented, but there are also paintings by Rembrandt, Van Dyke and others.

The surrounding gardens are well worth a visit, with beautiful gardens, woodland walks and a spectacular water garden designed by Harold Peto.

Eaton Weir

Onwards to Eaton Weir which boasts a pretty rustic bridge but no weir. This was the site of the last of the old "flash weirs" of the Thames and was removed in 1936.

The lock system that we have today is something that is generally taken for granted, but how did they develop?

It is believed that the first dams across the rivers in Britain were made by the Vikings, who during their raids overcame the problems of shallow water stranding their boats by building dams to raise the water level.

A more peaceful use was to provide millers with a sufficient head of water to drive their wheels. Fishermen too made use of artificial weirs to set traps across the river that gave them increased catches. Both of these helped to keep the water deep enough for boats, but there was one major problem. It may have made it easier to move the boats through the deeper waters, but when the craft reached the next weir it came to a sudden stop. There was no way through.

Someone, somewhere, must have been the first to come up with the bright idea that what was needed was a removable section of the dam wall. Take the section away, pass the boat through, put the section back again and away you go. Such must have been the thought process that gave us the "flash lock".

The early lock gate was a paddle of boards that were pressed by the current of the water against upright boards known as "rymers". When a boat wanted to travel downstream the paddles would be removed and a flash of water would take the vessel over the weir in the style of shooting the rapids. When the torrent had died down any boat wanting to travel upstream would be hauled up through the gap by either a team of horses or gang of men. Some of the bigger locks used a capstan to ease their toils.

This was not an easy operation to undertake. It was hazardous to say the least, and to perform the maneuvers successfully required great experience, skill and strength. The removal of the paddles in a speedy manner without also removing ones fingers was not always achieved. Boats shooting the weir must have been a spectacular sight and the adrenaline would have been really pumping through the veins of those whose task it was to steer the vessel down to calmer waters. Timing was everything. Removing the paddles too slowly would result in the water levels dropping too soon with the boat being grounded in the upstream section, and no doubt strong words were exchanged on such occasions.

William Morris

The small village of Kelmscott along with its splendid Elizabethan Manor House attracts me to take a short diversion to take a closer look, for one man described this place as his own "Heaven on earth".

That man was William Morris, who fell in love with the Manor House at first sight, and lived there from 1871 until his death in 1896. He would habitually wander the fields collecting reeds and flowers to use as dyes and patterns for his textile work.

Morris was a massive influence in Victorian times, not only as a designer and manufacturer but also as a radical political thinker. He was a founder of the Arts and Crafts Movement and a committed member of the Socialist League.

William was originally an Essex boy, born in Walthamstow in 1834. He spent his schooldays at Marlborough School and then attended Exeter College, Oxford. It was at Exeter College that he met the artist Edward Burne-Jones who would become his life-long friend and business partner.

His original career plan was to enter the church, but his readings of the social commentaries of Ruskin and Carlyle influenced him to join the arts world instead. After graduating from Oxford Morris worked for the architect George Street who specialised in Gothic Revivalist styling. There he met another person who would later contribute to his later works, Philip Webb. Morris soon moved from architecture to explore the world of painting under the tutelage of Dante Gabriel Rosetti.

It was to Philip Webb that Morris turned when he wanted to build a new house in Bexley Heath. He commissioned his friend to design the building in a simple vernacular style using traditional materials. It was at this point that Morris's life was to take a turn and leave us with the wonderful heritage of his works.

Try as he might, Morris just could not find the furniture and textiles to decorate his new home. Having been dragged around DFS and IKEA by my own dearly-beloved on many occasions on a similar mission I know exactly how frustrated he must have been. Our brains must have something in common, for we both came to the same conclusion – "We can do it ourselves". The results however could not have been more different. I ended up with a few wonky shelves and shapeless curtains, while Morris produced outstandingly fine works of art that were the envy of everyone

It is but a short distance to the next logical step. In true "Del-Boy" style he must have thought along the lines of "We can flog this stuff and this time next year we will all be millionaires". Morris with his socialist tendencies probably did not think exactly that thought but it must have been pretty close. With his friends Burne-Jones, Rosetti and Webb he formed Morris and Company with the purpose of selling the products they designed to the general populace.

The company blossomed and flourished under Morris's inspired leadership. Demand for its products soared. The products ranged through stained glass, textiles, soft furnishings, furniture and wallpaper. Many of the designs were based on the natural shapes of the flowers and foliage he collected at Kelmscott.

Morris remained a staunch socialist despite his entrepreneurial successes. He detested mechanisation and mass-production and insisted that his products were made by hand. His aim was to restore the values of traditional hand craftsmanship to all of his works and encourage others to do likewise.

There was an unfortunate paradox to his ambitions. The fine work he was producing by hand was too expensive to be affordable to any but the rich and the ordinary "man in the street" was unable to purchase such wonderful works.

Today the influence of Morris remains with us, and there are dedicated followers of his work. He rests in St Georges Churchyard at Kelmscott, at peace in his own "heaven on earth".

Radcot Bridge

The river straightens up as I approach Radcot, and the bridge is visible for quite a distance. However, as I draw closer other bridges appear in view. The various developments over the ages at Radcot have resulted in a chain of three bridges crossing three different streams of the waterway.

Radcot means "cottage by the road" and is mentioned in the Domesday Book as a two family unit with 24 acres of farmland. The ultimate owner was recorded as the King as was the common trend at the time.

There has been a bridge of some sorts at Radcot since the 10th century, but the first stone bridge was completed in 1225 and parts of this still stand to make this the oldest "proper" bridge across the Thames. The only craftsmen in those days who had the necessary skills to perform the task were attached to the religious houses, so the builders were probably monks from nearby Faringdon.

Radcot grew in importance as a consequence of the construction industry. Buildings were designed to look imposing and boost the prestige of those who lived in them. The finest buildings demanded the finest materials and there was no stone finer for this purpose than Taynton or Burford stone. There was just one small difficulty; the stone was in West Oxfordshire and the elegant buildings were planned for Oxford and London. The most efficient way of transporting the large quantities of stone required was by barge and the nearest waterway to the quarries was the Thames at Radcot so it was here that the wharves were built.

In the beginning simple wooden wharves were built and the stone loaded on to lighters that would take their cargo downstream to Oxford and then transferred to larger vessels to continue the voyage to London.

Such was the demand from the Oxford Colleges and the stately buildings of London for this stone that this means of transportation was insufficient and the answer was to use bigger boats.

Bigger boats required bigger wharves, so a canal was dug out to accommodate them and two new bridges were made, Canal Bridge and Pidnell Bridge, making the current chain of three.

For a tiny place Radcot has had more than its fair share of what today's media would call "incidents".

It is fair to say that Stephen was not our most popular King. Some would go further and say that he was the worst King we have ever had bar none. When you look closely at some of the other candidates for this award Stephen must have been a total washout to deserve this accolade. Matilda, Countess of Anjou, certainly thought so, and spent much of her time campaigning to depose him. Part of her plan involved setting up an earthworks castle in 1141 at Radcot causing travelers to make a wide detour. Whether this had any effect on Stephen as he sat enthroned in London doing his reigning is unknown, but it must have irritated the hell out of the weary traveler.

Things warmed up considerably during the reign of Richard II, who was one of those monarchs who seems to have been chasing after Stephen's "worst King", title. Richard was involved in a real family ding-dong with his relatives as they fought to influence him in his running of the country. This bickering faction was mainly composed of Richard's uncles and collectively known as the "Lords Appellant". Richard's chief adversary was Thomas of Woodstock who was the Duke of Gloucester. He managed to persuade Richard that his favourite uncle, Robert de Vere, Earl of Oxford, was plotting against him. De Vere heard about the plot and fled to the midlands where he drew together an army of 15,000 men and marched them southwards. His plan was to reinforce the Kings troops and then to show Gloucester the error of his ways and teach him a lesson.

Gloucester responded by advancing northward with a much larger army to intercept De Vere's forces. This action forced de Vere to take avoiding actions and take a diversion via Radcot. De Vere arrived at Radcot on the 19th of December 1387 and promptly found that his situation had deteriorated drastically because the Earl of Derby, Henry Bolingbroke (who would later become Henry IV) had taken his troops to guard the bridge to prevent De Vere advancing any further. To make matters worse Bolingbroke had removed the centre arch of the bridge to make sure that De Vere's army could not cross the river and so would be forced to fight. The ensuing battle was very one-sided.

Put yourselves in the position of De Vere's men. In front of you lies a broken bridge plus a lot of very aggressive men poking pikestaffs in your face. Behind them are a battalion of archers who look as though they mean business. Look to the north and all you can see are the rapidly advancing superior forces of Gloucester's army. What do you do?

Scarper; that's what.

De Vere joined them, forcing his horse to leap into the river to help him make his getaway. Amazingly he succeeded and eventually made his way to France where he later died in exile.

Gloucester and Bolingbroke naturally made the most of their victory. They returned to London and with the other Lords Appellant wrested control from the King and were able to condemn many of Richard's allies to an untimely end.

The bridge was repaired in 1393 and a monument for the battle was positioned on the bridge. Unfortunately this monument has since become lost.

More than two hundred and fifty years later the bridge was again the scene of a major incident. During the Civil War Royalist forces captured the bridges and established a garrison at nearby Radcot House. This helped to protect the supply route to loyalist Oxford. The Royalists held out against the Parliamentarians despite severe losses, but finally, in May 1646 the bridge was recaptured and as consequence Oxford fell to the Roundheads.

Quite a lot happened here in days gone by. You would not think it from the peaceful air that exists on this sunny spring morning. The only activity is a few people pottering about on their boats moored by the banks, and a lonely walker making his way along the towpath.

Radcot to Tadpole Bridge

This area of Oxfordshire is very flat, with the result that even minor intrusions into the skyline seem to have a more striking effect than they would otherwise merit. Even making allowances for the terrain the curved outline of Old Man's Bridge stands out impressively against the grey skies as I walk towards it.

In days gone by there used to be a weir at this spot. It was known as Old Man's Weir, or sometimes alternatively as Harper's Weir. This weir was in a very convenient location for travelers wishing to pass between Faringdon on the south side of the river and Bampton on the north, and it became a popular crossing point. When the weir was removed in the mid 1800's a footbridge was built to preserve the right of way across the water. The original bridge fell into a state of disrepair and was replaced by the present bridge in 1894.

The bridge itself is steep and very narrow with only enough width for a single person. Presumably this was to prevent traders from using this bridge for carts and thus enabling them to avoid the tolls at the main bridges further upstream at Radcot.

Old Man's Bridge is seemingly in the middle of nowhere, and its loneliness adds to the beauty. There is a certain ambience to this location and everything seems to fit together perfectly. I sit for a while to absorb the atmosphere and watch the waters glide beneath the wooden structure, the reflection adding to the symmetry of the scene.

Some old friends return as I step along the pathway. The meanders are back; and back in style. Together we twist and loop and turn, performing a choreographed dance across the meadows. Somewhere ahead is Rushey Lock, but is it in front or to the left or the right? The river moves left and right in deception and appears to be deliberately inducing a sense of giddiness until suddenly I cross the weir and arrive at Rushey Lock.

The weir at Rushey is of the old style "rhymer and paddle" construction, and the old paddles are stacked against the fence immediately before the weir. As I cross the weir the handles of the submerged paddles can be clearly seen on my left. This is one of the last weirs of this design still in use today.

Rushey Lock is very well kept with bright flower gardens and a superb foliage frog in the middle of the lawn, with its bulbous blue eyes keeping watch over the lock. I almost trip over the similarly constructed floral snail standing beside the lock-keeper's wooden hut.

After the gyrations of the previous section it is disappointing to find that the next stretch follows the lock access road in a relatively straight line to Tadpole Bridge. It is starting to rain as well. This would normally dampen my spirits, but a key destination point lies at the end of the track, then it can rain all it likes for a while. I am nearing the Trout Inn at Tadpole Bridge and that means lunch.

Tadpole Bridge itself is a bit of a disappointment. After the fine old stone bridges I have encountered upstream this one is rather plain. A simple single span standard stone bridge that is purely functional with none of the medieval beauty of Radcot or Lechlade.

In complete contrast immediately next to the bridge is the Trout Inn. This inn is everything that the bridge is not. Elegant and stylish, it also exudes a rustic charm that gives it a unique character.

The Trout has so many listings in various "good food and drink" guides that it seems almost ill-mannered to ask for a baguette. But rather like the adverts for Marks & Spencer's, this was no ordinary baguette; it is a Trout Inn baguette. A Thai sticky beef curry baguette to be precise. Delicious.

Suitably refreshed it is time to move on. The rain has momentarily stopped so that when I leave the cheerful bar of The Trout it is into that refreshing ozone-filled air that exists after the rains have stopped. Combined with the satisfaction of a very tasty lunch this gives me a "feel-good" high and I stuff the waterproof into my pack and look forward to the afternoon. Invigorated I walk on, but it is only a short while before the rain comes again and the waterproofs are pulled back out to resume their duties that last for the remainder of the day.

The path runs alongside the edge of one of the largest areas of natural meadowland in Britain. Chimney Meadow Nature Reserve covers 250 hectares of wildlife rich land and is managed by the Berks, Bucks and Oxon Wildlife Trust. The wetland supports large numbers of ground-nesting birds, and is a haven for rarer wading birds. Redshank, curlew and snipe have all been spotted here. The area is threaded with old waterways and hedgerows. The Trust has a program to restore more wildlife to Chimney Meadows over the coming years.

Tenfoot Bridge is a slightly smaller version of Old Man's Bridge. It is another narrow, lonely footbridge apparently situated in the middle of nowhere. Why Tenfoot Bridge when it is twelve feet high? Well, in similar manner to its look-alike the footbridge stands in a position that until 1870 was formerly occupied by a weir. This was referred to as Tenfoot Weir because when the paddles were removed the gap was ten feet wide.

Shifford

Shifford Lock Cut was opened in 1898. The natural river looped south to the village of Duxford and then back again. The idea of the cut was not just to save one and a half miles of journey time, but to avoid the shallow waters of Duxford that were preventing many vessels from travelling further upstream, forcing them to turn and go back to Newbridge. That the whole project only took eighteen months from conception to opening showed the urgency that this project was seen to have.

Legend has it that King Alfred held a witan or English Parliament at Shifford in 890. Looking around at the surrounding countryside you could not imagine such a thing happening today. It would surely keep down the bills for "expenses" because there is nothing to spend them on. In fact, what a good idea. Get the MPs to stand around in an empty field. It would be a lot cheaper.

There is some debate among historical scholars as to whether or not this event actually took place. The only record of such an occasion is to be found in a 12th Century poem, "The Proverbs of Alfred" where the place name is given as "Sifford". The whole thing may be fiction rather than fact. There is also an awkward historical point that this part of Oxfordshire did not come under Wessex administration until 910AD which is a little inconvenient for proving the story of a Witan being held in 890.

Newbridge

Newbridge takes its name from what Basil Fawlty would have called "the bleeding obvious". It is the new bridge, so called because it is "new" compared to Radcot Bridge which was completed about 25 years earlier. The bridge has six arches over the river, and six more each with a medieval pointed profile. The construction was instigated by the personal command of King John (who was yet another of those "bad kings") who wanted to speed up the transportation of wool from the Cotswolds. He probably was more interested in speeding up his ability to levy higher taxes on the wool merchants than for their profitability, but he did get the bridges built.

The weather is still miserable. It has rained ever since I left the Trout some two hours ago and it does not look like stopping. These are not the best conditions for viewing anything or taking photographs which is a great shame. Newbridge takes a marvelous photograph under the right conditions, but for now I have to imagine the honey-coloured stones glowing in the sun, with the pointed arches forming perfect reflections in the smooth waters.

Such thoughts lead to an admiration of the skills of those fine yeomen of Olde England who erected this magnificent structure for our enjoyment. What talents we had in England then; the best in the world.

Except they weren't - they were French.

The monks of Deerhurst Priory, near Gloucester were thought to have been the builders of the bridge. The local manor of La Nore (Northmoor) at the time belonged to the Priory so this connection is reasonably straightforward. Then we get a little more complicated. Edward the Confessor had made Deerhurst into an outpost of the Benedictine Priory of St Denis near Paris. It was from St Denis that the Pontife Brothers, notable ecclesiastical architects of their day, travelled to England in the first half of the 13th Century and influenced the construction of many buildings. The monks of Deerhurst became much sought after for their masonry skills and it is reasonable to assume that the Pontife Brothers had an influence over them.

Deerhurst Priory continued to maintain the bridge for just over 200 years, collecting tolls and carrying out repairs as necessary. This came to an end in 1460 when during the Hundred Years War the manor of La Nore was seized from the French and once again became the property of the Crown.

Similar to Radcot, the Cavaliers and Roundheads had a bit of a set-too here as well. Newbridge was situated right on the border between the two warring factions. It was conveniently halfway between Abingdon and Witney, Oxford and Faringdon, where the rivers Thames and Windrush conjoined, and was the "Checkpoint Charlie" of the day with the river forming a natural barrier. In 1644 the Roundhead commander, William Waller attempted to cross the river in order to lay siege to Oxford and capture King Charles but was thwarted by the Royalist forces. The King was safe for a while, but this was only a delay, Oxford eventually fell and the Roundheads claimed the country.

While we can easily accept that Newbridge was built after Radcot Bridge, the arguments rage about which is the oldest stone bridge across the Thames. For a start, Radcot Bridge, or at least the old part of it, does not actually cross the Thames. Since the rerouting of the river in 1787 the main stream passes under the extension to the bridge.

There is also the small matter that Radcot Bridge was not a bridge during the War of the Roses because Henry Bolingbroke took the middle piece away, so the present bridge has only been in place since its first restoration.

It is still raining. The pathway all too conveniently leaves the riverbank and enters the beer garden of The Maybush. It is so easy to follow the well-trodden route towards the entrance door and when I reach it some invisible and irresistible force-field drags me into the bar and orders a pint of Guinness.

DAY FOUR

NEWBRIDGE TO OXFORD

14.0 Miles

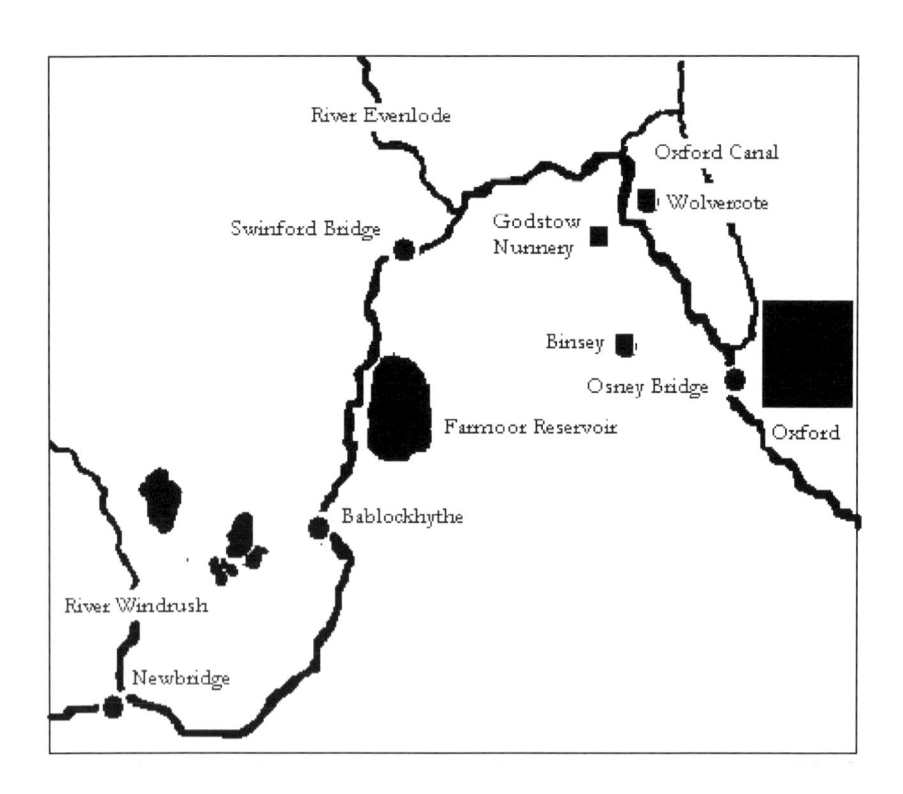

Bablock Hythe

Newbridge to Abingdon is not far by road, just a matter of 8 miles. The river is taking the scenic route and it will take me the best part of a day and a half. When the young Thames was cutting its way towards the sea it decided against taking the short straight line directly eastwards, but instead set off to the north and looped itself around the high ground of Cumnor and Wytham Hill. So it is northwards through the garden of "The Rose Revived" and on towards Oxford.

The next inn I come to is somewhat different. The Trout, The Maybush and The Rose Revived have all been ancient inns with local stone facades beaming their rustic welcome. By contrast the Ferryman Inn at Bablock Hythe is a stark building that could be described as "Art Deco" if you wanted to be polite, or "Council Estate" if you didn't. It is certainly not the prettiest building I have come across so far on this expedition, but with only a fifth of the route under my belt I am sure it will not be the ugliest either. I was to discover some ten days later that it would probably win architectural awards in parts of Deptford. There is a rather nice beer-garden area right on the riverbank which gets very busy during the summer.

The inn marks one of the most ancient crossing points of the Thames. The Romans are believed to have used this section to ford the river. There is evidence of a ferry here from at least 1279, when it was operated by John Cocas and the area was known as "Babbelak". Cocas operated the ferry under a rental agreement with Deerhurst Priory, who seemed to have something of a monopoly on river crossings around here in those days.

My way forward is obstructed by a large caravan and chalet park and I have to take a detour along the local roads and tracks before rejoining the river about a mile further downstream opposite Farmoor Reservoir.

Swinford Bridge

Two bridges across the Thames still levy tolls. The first of these is Swinford Bridge, which is also known as Eynsham Bridge. It was commissioned by the Earl of Abingdon in 1769 and is constructed in fine Georgian style with elegant circular arches and fine balustrades.

There has been a crossing here for over 1000 years. The name Swinford is allegedly a diminutive of Swine Ford.

The origins of the bridge are rumoured to date back to a time when King George III became stuck in the surrounding mud during a period of flood, and demanded that the Earl of Abingdon build a bridge for the convenience of travelers, or more truthfully for the benefit of the King if ever he travelled that way again. When the earl of Abingdon protested that such a bridge would be too expensive to build the King replied that he could charge tuppence a time to cross it and so it would pay for itself. This is exactly what followed, and the toll remained at two pennies from the day it was opened until we changed to decimal currency in 1971 when it became two new pence. An Act of Parliament in 1994 was required to change it to the princely (or should that be Kingly?) sum of five new pence which is the tariff that still remains in force today.

In the early days a dozen or so carriages would use the bridge each day and collecting tolls was not exactly arduous. The estimated usage figure today is approximately 3 million vehicles per year so the present toll keeper is definitely kept a lot busier than any of his predecessors.

From Swinford Bridge the river starts its long 180 degree bend that will take it around Wytham Hill and Wytham Woods and eventually to the dreaming spires of Oxford.

The apex of the curve is at Kings Weir Lock, where there is a connection to the Oxford Canal that lays only a couple of fields to the east. This is the farthest north that the Thames ventures during its journey, and we both slowly move southwards from here towards the sea.

Godstow

The path takes me underneath the busy A34 trunk road, and the dainty stone bridge at Godstow gradually appears into view.

I stand on the bridge and look across at one of "The" pubs along the banks of the Thames. This is the Trout Inn at Godstow and it has one of the finest riverside terraces you could desire for sitting in the sunshine with a drink and watching the river go by.

The small weir just upstream makes the waters running past the terrace an extremely attractive environment for fish. A large shoal of chub inhabits this stretch and the fish can often be seen cruising just below the surface, waiting for the inevitable piece of sandwich to be thrown towards them which rapidly disappears in a quick swirl. A very attractive wooden footbridge connects the terrace to an island in the river, although public access is not permitted.

The Trout was originally a hospice for the nearby Godstow Nunnery, and is believed to date from 1138. It was always a popular venue for the people of Oxford, and when it was featured regularly in the popular "Inspector Morse" books and television series it became very busy indeed.

I cross the narrow lane carried over the river by Godstow Bridge, and ahead lay the sad ruins of Godstow Nunnery.

Godstow was once a magnificent ecclesiastical complex. In addition to the nunnery it possessed a church, chapel, courtyards, cloisters, priest house, guest house and a chapter house. Now all that remains are the outer walls and ruins of the chapel.

The grounds were given to Edith, the widow of Sir William Launceline in 1133. Edith caused the priory to be built on what was then an island between two Thames streams. The nunnery was consecrated in 1139 to the honour of St.Mary and St John the Baptist.

How did the nunnery become so impressive? For that we must go back to one of the earliest Royal scandals.

Rosamund Clifford was a noted beauty of the 12th century. Known as "The Fair Rosamund" she first met and enchanted Henry II at her father's castle in 1163 when Henry was leading regular raids into Wales. She became his mistress, and when this eventually became public knowledge in 1164 there followed the inevitable rows between Henry and his wife, Eleanor of Aquitaine.

After two more years as Henry's mistress Rosamund decided to retire and join the sisterhood at Godstow Nunnery. Shortly after joining the community of nuns Rosamund died in what we would today cautiously term "suspicious circumstances". The detailed facts are not recorded or properly known, but suffice to say that the popular conspiracy theory of the day included the words "poison" and "Eleanor".

Rosamund was buried in front of the high altar at Godstow. King Henry was distraught, and granted large endowments to the nunnery in memory of Rosamund. These endowments were utilised to expand the properties to their later glory.

The local people had taken Rosamund to their hearts and decorated the tomb with flowers and it became a shrine for many years. Then, in 1191, two years after Henry II's death, the Nunnery received a visit from the Bishop of Lincoln. On seeing the shrine in front of the high altar the bishop denounced Rosamund as a harlot and ordered the shrine to be destroyed and the body exhumed and reinterred outside of the church. The second grave was still visited by many of the local people who paid tribute until it was destroyed during the dissolution in 1539.

The nunnery also had a somewhat racy reputation. An information board at Godstow Lock coyly refers to its former reputation for offering "hospitality" to the monks of Oxford.

After the dissolution, the nunnery was turned into a private residence by George Owen and became known as Godstow House. The civil war brought the final destruction of the former nunnery with constant clashes between Royalists and Roundheads. After this the stones were taken away by local people to build their houses, leaving the sad, grey outlines that we see today.

Some say that the fair Rosamund is still to be found wandering the ruins and surrounding meadow as the Ghost of the Grey Lady soulfully searching for her final resting place and everlasting peace.

Charles Dodgson

It would be too much to hope that a white rabbit carrying a large pocket-watch and yelling "I'm late, I'm late I'm late", would race across my path as I wandered across Godstow meadow. Popular myth has it that one did many years ago, on July 4th 1862 and famously became the start of that favourite children's book, "Alice in Wonderland".

Godstow was a favourite place for Charles Dodgson, better known to us as the writer Lewis Carroll. Dodgson was a lecturer in mathematics at Christ Church College where he spent all of his adult life. He became a close friend of the Dean of Christ Church College, Henry Liddel, and his wife Lorina. On a summers day Charles liked nothing more than to take a boat and row the four young Liddel children, Harry, Lorina, Edith and Alice up the river to Godstow meadow for a picnic, and entertain them by telling them stories.

Dodgson was brilliant with words, which coupled with his vivid imagination produced stories that delighted the children. They were always demanding more stories and encouraged him to write them down so they could read them again for themselves. Charles Dodgson is widely recognised to have invented many word games, including an early form of scrabble and word ladders, where one letter is changed at a time to turn one word into another, e.g. cat – cot – dot – dog.

Dodgson was a very clever man, not just skilled in the use of words but a highly intelligent thinker, logician, mathematician and photographer. Among his inventions was the postal order, an electoral system for proportional representation, double-sided tape, a device for justifying margins on a typewriter, and (most usefully to my mind), a simple cardboard scale device that when held next to a beer glass could easily check that you had been served the correct measure. This gizmo became immediately popular among the common rooms of Oxford University.

Not a good day for picnics today. The rain keeps coming and in the absence of white rabbits it is onward to the city of dreaming spires that I can see in the distance across the fields.

The Treacle Well

I want to take a short detour to view the treacle well. "Fancy falling for that one" I hear you chuckle. Chuckle ye not, for the "Treacle Well" does indeed exist and can be found in the churchyard of St Margaret's Church at Binsey.

Treacle was an old English word for medicine, and was also used to describe dark coloured undrinkable water, which from its foul palate was associated with the commonly held taste of medicine. Consequently a well where the water became undrinkable would be termed a "treacle well".

A more romantic story is attached to this particular well, which is situated by the small Binsey church that at one time used to be a part of the Priory of St Frideswide.

Frideswide was a Saxon princess who was born around 650AD. She was the daughter of Didanus and his wife Safrida. Frideswide took holy orders as a nun and made her vows of celibacy. Nonetheless Frideswide was pursued by King Agar of Mercia who was eager to marry her and establish stronger bonds with the Saxon tribes. Frideswide rejected his unwanted advances and ran away, hiding herself in the woods. Agar did not take too kindly to his rejection, and brought an army to Oxford to claim his prize by means of force. To save Frideswide from her unwanted fate, so the story goes, Agar was struck blind before he was able to complete his mission.

Frideswide heard about the blindness and for some unaccountable reason took pity on Agar, praying fervently that his sight should be restored. She prayed especially to St Margaret of Antioch. St. Margaret had lived during the time that the Romans were persecuting the Christians and in common with Frideswide she had attracted the advances of an unwelcome suitor and likewise chose to flee to safety. The spurned admirer sought his revenge for this perceived slight by denouncing Margaret as a Christian to the authorities. The result was that Margaret was arrested, tried, found guilty and beheaded.

During one of her prayers to St Margaret, Frideswide heard a voice from the heavens telling her to strike the ground nearby with her staff. She followed the instructions and when she beat the ground with her staff the earth opened up and revealed a small well. Frideswide took some of the water from the well and bathed Agar's eyes in the fluid, with the result that his sight was miraculously restored. To mark the miracle Frideswide established her priory next to the well and dedicated the chapel to St Margaret of Antioch.

I return to the river via "The Perch" which is another excellent riverside pub, with a garden leading me back down to the river.

Oxford

It is a lovely walk along this part of the Thames. The open grazing land of the Binsey meadows, dotted with bushes and trees, with the famous row known as the "Binsey Populars" by the waterside. Across on the opposite bank is the wide-open expanse of Portmeadow, separating the river from the city. Portmeadow was bequeathed to the commoners of Wolvercote by William the Conqueror, and the descendants of those early villagers still have the common grazing rights today. The famous "Dreaming Spires" of the churches and university buildings can be clearly seen jutting into the skies beyond the meadow.

The first college at Oxford was University College which was founded in 1249. This was quickly followed by Balliol College and Merton College in 1263 and 1264 respectively. There are currently 38 colleges and 7 religious Permanent Private Halls that make up the University of Oxford today. Until 2008 there were 39 Colleges, but two of the colleges, Green College and Templeton College merged. This was the first ever merger of two Oxford colleges. Oxford University contains some of the most intelligent and sophisticated brains in England, so what, do you imagine, did these super-humans with brains the size of a planet come up with as a name for this newly conjoined seat of learning? Yes indeed; Green Templeton College.

The river at Oxford divides into many smaller streams that rejoin later to carry their waters downstream to London. There are also many side-streams that join the river at Oxford. These, plus the River Cherwell combine to ensure that there is roughly twice the quantity of water in the river as it leaves Oxford as there is when it first enters the city.

I pass the Medley Sailing Club and Bossoms Boatyard, and cross over the red "Rainbow Bridge" that marks the start of the Oxford Channel. The towpath alongside the channel is very popular with walkers and can become quite crowded on summer weekends. It is a delightful walk, with tree-lined banks on both sides.

The walk through the trees ends at a large basin where the Oxford Canal joins the river. The Oxford Canal is one of our most picturesque inland waterways, linking the Grand Union Canal from a point just north of Coventry with the River Thames. This link enabled coal from the Warwickshire coalfields to be brought to Oxford.

The canal today is very popular with holiday-makers, particularly the southern part between Oxford and Banbury. Along this popular section the canal follows the River Cherwell and the railway line, the three of them often within a few steps of each other.

I cross the canal bridge, and a few minutes later I am standing at Osney Bridge which has the honour of being the lowest bridge on the navigable river. In fact it is so low that it is inadvisable to stand up on a boat going under the bridge unless you wish to receive a very nasty bang on the head. The low clearance is the main reason that the larger river cruisers are not often seen upstream of Oxford because they can not pass under the bridge.

This is the end of my walk for today. Tomorrow the boats will be bigger, and the river will continue to grow bigger too. The loneliness and isolation of the first four days will start to fade. Villages will come closer to the bank of the river and the scenery will change once again.

DAY FIVE

OXFORD TO SHILLINGFORD

20.6 Miles

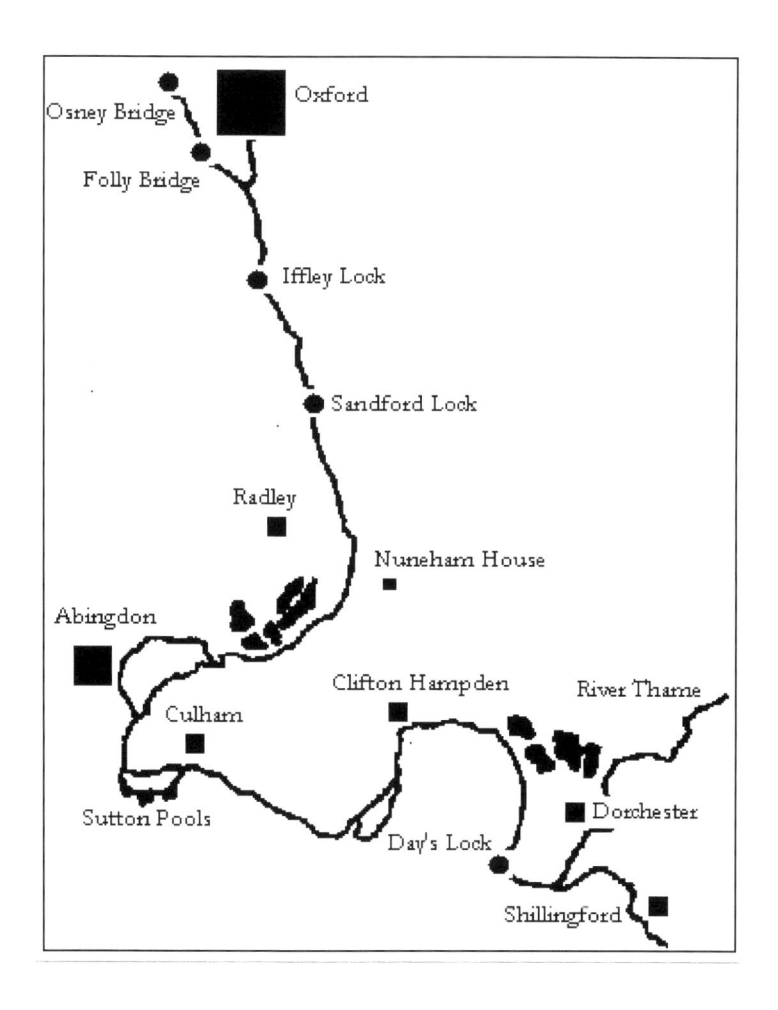

Osney Bridge to Folly Bridge

I have been looking forward to today's walk. The only thing going against me is the rain. I don't know it yet, but as well as the longest day of my walk it is also going to be the wettest. To be fair it only rained once, but it kept coming down in bucketfuls for six hours.

Today I will be covering the longest distance that I plan to complete in a single day, being just a fraction less than twenty-one miles. It is not however the distance that is the major attraction for me. The Thames now passes through what I consider to be its best setting, where the mighty river seems to me to be at the most balanced stage of its development. Everything seems to be in proportion and simply just "right".

The waters have widened to form an ideal relationship with bank-side trees and buildings. No more the narrow confines of the upper reaches, or the wide expanses of the lower river that make the far-bank trees, bushes and even buildings appear rather distant. The vast majority of the day will be spent still walking through natural meadows, before prepared and maintained paths become more frequent. Buildings too are situated in that "in-between" state. The loneliness of the isolated farms that kept their distance from the upper river will be slowly disappearing as the habitation creeps steadily towards the river. Today the river will just tentatively venture into the outskirts of the city of Oxford and lightly kiss the edges of Abingdon. It is as if the river is playing out a courtship ritual with urban development before taking the plunge and becoming part of the "town set" in the stew pot of water, tarmac and brick that make up the lower sections.

Immediately below Osney Bridge the Thames pathway passes the first industrial area it has encountered so far on the route. However, this is only a short walk and I am soon at the Grandpont Nature Reserve. This area has been carefully recovered from an old gasworks site and it is steadily reverting back to its natural state. The only evidence that can be seen of its former industrial occupation are the elegant white-painted "gasworks bridges" that cross the river. Nowadays they are apparently going nowhere, but in their working days they would have carried the numerous coal trucks that kept the city's gasworks in full production.

Folly Bridge looms up out of the miserable rain. There has been a crossing here since time immemorial, and it is probably this point that was the original ox ford that later gave the city its name. The first bridge dated from Saxon times and was constructed from timber. It was replaced with a stone built bridge by the early Normans around 1085, when it became known as South Bridge or Grand Pont. During the 13th century a nearby house was occupied by the Franciscan Friar, Roger Bacon, who was an early alchemist and astronomer at the University. Bacon was believed to have been the cause of the bridge at one time being named Friars Bridge, a name it kept until the end of the English Civil War.

After the Civil War the building was taken over by a Mr. Welcome, who added an extra storey. This resulted in the building having a pronounced top-heavy appearance, making it seem to everyone who looked at it that it was about to topple over. Some local wag then christened it "Welcome's Folly" and from that point in time it became generally known as Folly Bridge. The original building was demolished in 1779 but the name has stuck firm ever since.

Many people imagine that the name "Folly Bridge" arises from a neighbouring house known as Caudwell's Castle. This unique building has

65

an unusual castellated façade, with cast iron balconies and further embellished with statues fixed on the walls. However, my research revealed that this structure was not even in existence until 1849, so we must go back to Mr. Welcome as being primarily responsible for the name.

Shortly afterwards I pass Grandpont House. It was originally built for the town clerk, Sir William Elias Taunton, but it is a later resident that with a little imagination is potentially of much more interest. In the mid 1800's Grandpont House was occupied by Alderman Thomas Randall. Now Alderman Randall was not a popular man. He was a local magistrate and seemed to have spent a great deal of his time leading a campaign to restrict public house opening times. Quite understandably this did not endear him with many of the students in Oxford. Alderman Randall had made his wealth as a hatter (you may see where this tale is going now). Who do we know who liked to have a few snifters around the city hostelries during the mid 1800's? Yes indeed, Mr. Charles Ludwig Dodgson. It would be jolly good fun if he had immortalised the Alderman as his "Mad Hatter" in such a satirical fashion.

Thus cheered I stride through the raindrops, passing the mouth of the River Cherwell emptying its waters into the main river and making its contribution to the wider stretches of the river that lay ahead.

Donnington and Oxford University Boathouses

Downstream of Folly Bridge the river suddenly comes alive. It is only 8am but the various Colleges rowing crews have been hard at work for some time already, and are being put through their paces by enthusiastic and vociferous coaches. No doubt they are all working up a good appetite towards a hearty breakfast before a hard day studying.

Do those racing boats move! They skim through the water at speeds that motor vehicles caught up in the Oxford rush hour would consider sheer ecstasy. There are so many boats chasing up and down the river that how they manage to avoid collisions is a miracle. It is really quite amazing that there are not constant clashes of oars echoing across the morning air.

The coaches also seem to have their own invisible radar system to avoid collisions. They cycle furiously along the towpath seemingly not looking where they are going with their eyes firmly fixed on their particular team of heaving rowers while shouting a constant stream of advice and encouragement to exhort their protégés to even greater efforts.

For a rower it must be a huge advantage to your blood-pressure if you are somewhat deaf. All the while that you are heaving and straining on a giant oar, sweat pouring from your brow, some bloke on a bike is yelling at you to put some more effort in. Even worse, there you are, six feet four and sixteen stone of well-honed Adonis and at the same time you are also being screamed at by a seven stone midget wearing a baseball cap who is sitting at the front-end of the boat. I know that it would really wind me up.

To all of the rowing activity add a full procession of people along the towpath intermingling in both directions. There are people cycling to work, school or to the shops. There are more people on foot propelling themselves at different speeds, fit-as-a-butchers-dog runners, puffing joggers, walkers, dog walkers, pram pushers and one man plodding his way down the Thames Pathway watching everybody else around him. Ladbrokes must surely be offering short odds on a pile-up somewhere. But no, all too soon Iffley Lock comes and goes, the throb of activity gets left behind and it is out to open countryside for a peaceful ten miles to Abingdon.

Iffley Lock to Abingdon

Iffley Lock was the site of the first "Pound Lock" to be built on the Thames. It was constructed in 1631 by the Oxford-Burford Commission.

A pound lock was simply a forerunner of the system that we see today. A chamber with a gate at each end held firmly against its supports by the pressure of water from upstream. Sluices control the water level in the chamber, so by a combination of opening and closing these gates and sluices the water level in the chamber can be raised or lowered allowing vessels to continue on their journey.

The earliest known pound lock dates from 1373 and was on the River Lek in Holland.

Portcullis style gates were used by the Italians in the 1400s, and it was Leonardo Da Vinci who is believed to have introduced mitred gates with vertical inbuilt sluices for the San Marco Lock in Milan, completed in 1495. It was some while before the pound lock system was brought to England and used on the Exeter Ship Canal in 1564.

The Oxford-Burford Commission was responsible for the second and third pound locks on the Thames that I will shortly discover at Sandford and Swift Ditch, near Abingdon.

The current lock was rebuilt in 1924, and is commemorated by a small stone block bridge and landing stage.

I am indebted to a retired officer from the Thames Valley Constabulary for this next snippet, which he swears is true.

Iffley Lock had certain notoriety in the early 1960s as a suicide spot. At that time the lock sat on an administrative dividing line between three different coroners' jurisdictions. The lock itself came under Oxford City, and immediately below the lock the left-hand bank was administered by Oxfordshire Coroners Office and the right bank by Berkshire.

A payment was offered by the coroner of Berkshire of half a crown (2/6d) for every body that was recovered on his bank. The Oxfordshire coroner would only pay two shillings for bodies recovered on his, whilst the Oxford City coroner would pay nothing at all. I am reliably informed by the retired officer that by some remarkable coincidence all bodies retrieved from the lock were removed on the Berkshire bank, so miraculously generating the maximum reward for the boys in blue. On the other hand the Oxford City coroner enjoyed a far easier life because no bodies from the lock area were ever presented to him for examination.

As I continue my wanderings along the towpath I come across one of those little idiosyncrasies which seem to be there just because they are there. A kissing-gate and surround decorated with metallic fish. The fish are swimming across the gate. What is it doing here? Answers on a postcard please, because I have been unable to discover anything more about this gate.

Onwards to Sandford Lock which proudly boasts that it has the greatest fall of water between its gates (2.96m) on the river. The water crashing over the weir can be quite impressive on its day, and today is one of those days. The rain has swollen the river and the "Sandford Lasher" is in full force. In his book "Three Men in a Boat" Jerome K Jerome described the pool below the lasher as "A very good place to drown yourself in" and it is easy to see why. The water rushes over the weir, pounding itself into the pool below.

The stretch from Sandford to Abingdon is a return to the loneliness that prevailed before arriving at Oxford. The fields are open again, with the occasional copse breaking into the meadows. It's back to nature again, and I step out on a long steady southward curve that will take me to Abingdon.

Seemingly in the middle of nowhere there is a boathouse. The forecourt is filled with rowing boats of all sizes. This is the boathouse of Radley College; one of England's most celebrated public schools. One cannot help but compare the recreational facilities available to their pupils compared to those offered by the local comprehensive. An impressive boat house standing on the banks of England's finest river is a long way removed from the pot-holed basketball court of an inner city sink school. A similar thought was to pass my mind in a couple of days time as I approached Windsor. This time even Radley College would be considered to be comparative paupers, for Eton College possesses a far more impressive boathouse, not to mention being also the proud owners of their own rowing course alongside the Thames. It is so good that it has been chosen as the rowing venue for the 2012 Olympics.

Looking across the river I view one of the first examples of something that will become more frequent over the next few days, "Very Nice Houses".

This particular VNH is Nuneham House, which was built for the first Lord Harcourt. The grounds were beautifully landscaped, and Lord Harcourt even went to the extreme measure of having the local village moved so that Capability Brown could have a free rein to beautify the countryside to achieve perfection.

Abingdon

Approaching Abingdon I come to Swift Ditch, where the remains of the original lock can still be seen, and then cross the river by means of

Abingdon Lock. From the lock it is a short walk to the Abingdon Bridge, which although it has been mostly rebuilt over the years still retains its medieval appearance.

Once under the bridge I am able to view one of the classic scenes of the Thames. St Helens Church and almshouses command the far bank as they have done for many centuries. The church of St Helen dates from the 11th Century and the almshouses were added in the 14th century.

Abingdon is one of the oldest towns in England. A Benedictine Abbey was founded here in 695, and the present street market is said to have originated in 1086. In 1084 William the Conqueror brought his son, the future Henry I, to the Abbey to be educated.

Abingdon was once the county town of Berkshire, but its failure to adopt the railway culture during the nineteenth century left it struggling outside the mainstream of Victorian life, and the title was passed to the growing town of Reading in 1867. Jerome K Jerome simply described Abingdon as "boring".

Although Abingdon itself retains an air of antiquity, the same can not be said for its surrounding area which is a veritable hotbed of modern high technology. There are huge local science parks at Milton, Harwell and Culham, with the latest addition being the Diamond Light Source that is the UK's biggest scientific project for over 40 years.

Sadly, two of Abingdon's most famed enterprises have both closed. MG cars (Morris Garages) were manufactured here until 1980, and more recently the famous Morlands Brewery has also come to an end, although its most famous product "Old Speckled Hen" is still brewed in Bury St Edmunds by the current brand owners Greene King.

Open fields call again, and leaving Abingdon behind I am striding towards the idyllic villages of Sutton Courteney, Culham and Clifton Hampden.

Culham

Passing through a gate there seems to be something wrong. The river is clearly on my right and continues straight ahead for some distance and yet to my left, among the woodland greenery, stands a fine medieval river bridge. What is going on?

What has been going on is that throughout my journey through Abingdon I was not following the natural course of the river. From the time of leaving the remains of the old Swift Ditch Lock I have been following a channel cut by the monks during the middle ages. (Monks seem to have carried out a lot of the work on the upper Thames; their life was obviously not restricted to vespers and cloisters as is so commonly assumed).

The bridge I can see is Old Culham Bridge, which now only crosses the Swift Ditch and not the major navigation channel. Its original purpose is no longer served and so it is allowed to while away the years in sleepy semi-retirement.

Sadly Swift Ditch is not to be found on the present day Ordnance Survey map. At some point in time it has been "re-branded" and now parades itself as "Back Water", a name that seems to invoke a more down-market response than its predecessor.

The river continues ahead and twists its way through Sutton Pools, a series of ponds that lie between the main river and the picturesque village of Sutton Courteney. My path takes a ninety degree left hand turn and follows the Culham Cut, a cutting made at the start of the 19th century and opened in 1809 at the same time as Culham Lock.

The original need for the cut was a mixture of ease of use and economics. The natural route for boats through Sutton Pools involved a lot of difficult maneuvering, but also involved encountering a lock situated beside a mill. This lock, as a consequence of the effect of the pools, took a great deal of water to fill it, and so was costly in both time and money. Controversy was the order of the day with merchants and barge owners not at all happy about the high tolls charged by the mill owner. The Thames Navigation Commission made many unsuccessful attempts to reconcile the differences, but the complaints continued to pour in and they finally commissioned the construction of the new lock at Culham and made a cutting to bypass the contentious pools. This made everyone happy again. Well, almost everyone, because the miller was not happy one little bit. He had lost all of the revenue from his tolls.

The village of Culham has a lovely village green and Victorian church. In earlier times it gained importance when it became the main wharf for the transportation of stone from the demolished Abbey at Abingdon to be re-used for buildings in London.

Engineers have taken another loop out of the river by digging the Clifton Lock Cut. Following the great success of the Culham Cut, the Navigation Commission repeated the same trick a little further downstream at Clifton. Instead of following the natural course that twists through the village of Long Wittenham I am able to continue my steps in a steady curve along the Clifton Lock Cut. Shortly after I have passed by the lock the river starts to bend the other way and one of the most beautiful "chocolate-box" scenes along the whole river slowly reveals itself.

Clifton Hampden

The red brickwork of Clifton Hampden Bridge spans the river to form a majestic foreground. To my left the rooftops of the village peek through the wooded hillside, and pointing into the sky above the rooftops the spire of St Michael and All Angels puts the final touch to this delightful view.

How amazing it is that we have this wondrous scene. Well, no, as it happens. All that I can see before me was designed to give exactly the uplifting effect that it has achieved.

The designer was Sir Gilbert Scott (1811 to 1878) who is probably better known for designing the Albert Memorial that takes pride of place in Kensington Gardens. Scott was commissioned by the local Lord of the Manor, Henry Hucks Gibbs, (Lord Aldenham), to design the main features of the village that form the marvelous view before me. He designed not only the bridge, but also the Manor House and the renovation of the church. St Michaels and All Angels was originally constructed in the 13th century, but Scott completely redesigned and rebuilt it. He allegedly modeled the bridge on a medieval bridge that can be found to the south of Nantes in France.

Next to the bridge stands the Barley Mow, one of the best-known public houses along the river. Jerome K Jerome wrote of the Barley Mow *"without exception the quaintest, most old-world inn up the river (standing) on the right of the bridge, quite away from the village. Its low-pitched gables and thatched roof and latticed windows give it quite a story-book appearance, while inside it is even still more once-upon-a-timeyfied…"*

Unfortunately, at the date I was at Clifton Hampden the inn was closed for refurbishment, and I crossed back over the bridge to the small village post office in search of refreshment. There has been much hoo-hah over the closure of rural post offices in recent years, so finding one here was something of an accomplishment in itself. However, a step inside the door quickly reveals why it is still here. This is not a normal tiny post office; it is a tardis. Every nook and cranny was filled with provisions for both villagers and this weary walker. Chiller units held refreshing drinks and a wide choice of snacks. The postmaster could hardly move behind his tiny counter. Several shoppers came in while I pondered my choice of lunch, including a couple of builders who purchased a typical builders-fayre lunch, pork pies, apple pies, Mars bars and a 2 litre bottle of Diet Coke. Why do they always do that? The message of sensible eating must be getting through to them but only in a stuttering manner. "All this fat and sugar can't be good for us", they must think, "We must balance it up with a diet Coke and then we will be fine".

I pay for my sandwiches and full-calorie Tango and step back out into the rain. The builders are sitting in their van, munching their dietary dynamite in the snug, dry environment of their white Transit, while I trudge along looking for a sheltering tree under which I can partake of my recently acquired nourishment.

In my humble opinion the Thames below Clifton Hampden is one of the most beautiful stretches on the river. The far bank is covered with trees, with a few Very Nice Houses poking through the gaps. In late autumn the opposite bank becomes a changing canvas of browns, yellows and reds as Mother Nature makes preparations for her winter shutdown. At this time of year photographers abound along the pathway, all trying for the ultimate autumn scene, with trees and river combining to give unlimited permutations of colours and reflections.

Day's Lock, World Championship Venue

Several major sporting events are held each year on the waterway. Rowing has the Boat Race, Henley, Marlow and numerous other regattas. Later in the walk I will pass Craven Cottage, the home of Fulham Football Club. Now another major international sporting arena appears, Day's Lock Footbridge.

Day's Lock is the venue for the World Pooh-Sticks Championships. If you do not believe me go to www.pooh-sticks.com .

It all started in 1984 when the resident lock keeper, Lynn David, thought it would be a fun way to raise money for his favourite charity, the Royal National Lifeboat Institution. The event prospered and for the last few years it has been organised by the local Rotary Club of Sinodon with all proceeds going to charity.

The event is usually held on the last Sunday in March, and a worthy cause if you find yourself in the area. There is also a team championship, and in 2007 the winners came all the way from Japan to participate.

There are some things that just have to be done. If I was at Lords I would have to bowl an imaginary ball from the Nursery End, leap and spin in the air shouting my appeal to an imaginary umpire. If allowed onto the pitch at Wembley I would have to swerve up the pitch, aim a kick at the goal and rush towards the stands with arms raised. Here I step on to the bridge and drop a stick into the water, and turn to watch it appear on the other side of the bridge.

World Pooh Sticks Championship
Dateline; Sunday March 29th 2009

I simply had to return to Day's Lock the following spring to witness the great event for myself.

It was a good week-end for sport. England beat Slovakia 4-0 at Wembley, Oxford stormed past Cambridge to win the boat race and Jenson Button blasted his way around a Melbourne track to win the first Grand Prix of the season. All paled into insignificance in my diary because today is the day of the World Pooh Sticks Championship.

A pleasant walk from Dorchester to Day's Lock and I was among many hundreds of people who had flocked to this small part of Oxfordshire for a day of simple fun. You may imagine it's all for the kids, and indeed there were children around who all seemed to have brought their cuddly Pooh Bears, Piglets and Eeyores with them for the day. However there is more entertainment to be had from the various happy bands of "nutters" who can only be found in this mad country of ours. There seemed to be crazy teams from all over the place, complete with their logo T-shirts. I even spotted a team proudly claiming to represent Cambridge University, who had a great deal more success (and probably a great deal more fun) than eight of their fellow students had on the same day on the Thames between Putney and Mortlake.

The queue to obtain "sticks" from the grandly titled "Keeper of the Sticks" wound through the trees for at least fifty yards by the time I got there. Only having a relatively short time window I reluctantly gave up my chance of World Championship glory and I walked on to watch the team races that were already under way.

It was all reassuringly "low-tech". Even Ross Brawn may find it a challenge too far to fit a "go-faster" gizmo on a piece of painted stick, although I bet given half a chance he could come up with something that Ferrari would complain about.

The starter wore the ubiquitous "hi-vis" jacket and bellowed his instructions "Ready............Steady.........Drop!" and four contestants would drop their coloured sticks into the water on the upstream side of the footbridge, then twist around and shout encouragement to their stick as the current moved it towards the finish line.

The finish line continued with the low technology, and was made up of a blue rope stretched between the banks, with a finish line judge peering with great concentration along it to enable him to give the verdict awaited with excited anticipation some thirty or so paces back at the bridge. He would consult with his assistant before shouting "Red, green, blue, yellow", or whatever order the race had finished.

At the end of each race the sticks are retrieved. This operation was entertainingly carried out by six volunteers packed into an inflatable boat. Their task was to reach out into the water and gather the painted sticks for re-use.

One member of the "retrieval team" had discovered a novel way of collecting the sticks. Now, what implement would you select for doing this job? I suppose you have automatically said "a fishing net". Nothing so obvious for this fine fellow. He would lean right over the side of the inflatable and try to hook a yard broom over the stick and draw it toward the boat. This provided us spectators with much entertainment. As he leaned out over the water we would all look on in anticipation….will he….will he………will he? But no, he remained firmly in the boat.

Who won? I don't know because I had to leave before the end. I suspect very few cared who won anyway. The actual winner does not really matter. The true winners were the hundreds of people who had a day of simple fun in the early-spring sunshine.

What is in a Name?

The Thames above and around Oxford is often locally referred to as the "Isis". The origin of this name is shrouded in mystery. It does not appear to have carried this name in the days of the Romans or Saxons. In fact the name does not appear to have been used at all until the 14th century when it was referred to as "Isa".

There is some conjecture that the Roman name for the river, Tamesis was derived from joining "Isis" to "Thame", in recognition of the joining of the two rivers at Dorchester. A neat idea, seemingly with plenty of logic, apart from the all important minor detail that nobody called it the Isis until thirteen hundred years later!

The original naming of the river as the Isis has been attributed to students at the University. It is thought that they named it as a reference to Isis, the perfect mother of the ancient Egyptians, relating this to the river being the perfect mother of their University.

There is a further hypothesis that the name "Thames" is derived from the Sanskrit word "Tamasa" meaning dark water. This theory conveniently ignores the question of what the pre-historic locals would have called it before an early immigrant from the east came along to persuade them to name their waterway in a foreign tongue.

The most logical history of the name is, as these things often are, the most boring. The Britons are believed to call it Tems, which was latinised by the Romans to Tamesis by their scribes and recorders. The Anglo-Saxons, who made changes to everything Roman that they could, put their own spin-doctors to work and came up with the spelling of Tamyse. This seemed to suit everyone until sometime around 1600, when those who spend their administrative lives working out ways to change everything that people were previously quite happy with, came to the decision that the name would benefit from an added "H" and that the "Y" was a superfluous luxury that we could henceforth do without.

We may expect the Ordnance Survey to come to our assistance in this matter but it is not to be. Firmly sitting on the fence the custodians of all thing cartographic put "River Thames or Isis" on their maps to continue the mystery. In practice I have seldom heard anybody use the name Isis outside of Oxford.

All that said, I arrive at the footbridge at the confluence of the Thames (or Isis) and the River Thame and look down upon its waters.

Dorchester

Half a mile upstream on the Thame lays the village of Dorchester-on-Thames. If we are being truly accurate the village should be Dorchester-on-Thame. It is a pretty little place and steeped in history.

This area has been inhabited since the earliest times. On the opposite side of the Thames on the Sinodon hills once stood an early Iron Age fort, and more Ancient Britons are thought to be responsible for the Dyke Hills, a narrow strip of earthwork between the main river and the current village.

Dorchester's position made it a very attractive proposition as a secure location. The Romans thought so too, and built a fort with a network of ditches for added security. They called the settlement Dorcic and built a road to the military camp of Alchester (near to Bicester). Archaeologists have found many Roman remains in the area, including an inscribed altar stone.

It is when we delve into the Ecclesiastical world of our ancestors that we find the most interesting things about the history of Dorchester.

The relationships between the early Britons and Saxons were strained to say the least. Alliances constantly changed and they were forever plotting against each other. Pope Honorius I decided that the best way to sort out these warring factions would be to convert them all to Christianity. In 634 he sent one of his Bishops, a Frank by the name of Birinus to convert the Saxons of the Thames Valley to Christianity.

Birinus set about his task with great zeal and his fame spread. At this time the West Saxon King, Cyneglis, was trying to forge an alliance with Oswald King of Northumbria in order that they might get together and have a go at the Mercians. Oswald, however, was a devout Christian, and would not allow himself to be seen to be in partnership with a heathen. Seeing something of an opportunity here, Birinus wasted no time in persuading Cyneglis that his best career-move was to be baptized, and the ceremony took place in the waters of the Thame at Dorchester. As a token of his thanks Cyneglis gave Birinus the right to form the Diocese of Dorchester and he became the first Bishop of Dorchester. For a short time Dorchester even became the capital of Wessex but it was soon displaced by the much larger town of Winchester.

Birinus was very active and was reputed to have founded many churches in Oxfordshire, Berkshire and Buckinghamshire. When Cyneglis died, his successor King Cenwalh invited him to found a new church in Winchester.

Birinus was sainted, and his feast days are on December 4th in the Roman Catholic Church, and are commemorated on September 4th in the Church of England. The small Catholic Church dedicated to St Birinus is near to the present road bridge over the River Thame.

Things stayed pretty much as they were until 1085, when the Diocese was transferred to the control of the Diocese of Lincoln. It seems rather a long way to transfer control, but as I have seen before on this journey, people did seem to travel an awfully long way in those early days with only simple means of transport. What they would have got up to if they had developed the internal combustion engine would be anybody's guess.

Alexander, the Bishop of Lincoln, founded Dorchester Abbey in 1140 for the Augustinian Monks. It was richly endowed from the surrounding Parishes and had an income of £220 (a not-so-small fortune in those days) at the time that it was dissolved by Henry VIII in 1536.

The inside of the Abbey is filled with ornate carvings, monuments and magnificent stained glass windows. The most celebrated of these is the famous "Jesse Tree" window, a pictorial reference to the lineage of Jesus as foretold by the prophet Isaiah.

Shillingford

The short diversion over, I return to the confluence and continue downstream towards Shillingford. The pathway veers across to meet the main road and then takes me down the unadopted Wharf Road back towards the river. This small deviation throws up a couple of nice surprises.

Firstly there is Wisteria Cottage with its front covered for about fifty yards with blue Wisteria. It has obviously been lovingly tended for many years and is a most wonderful sight.

Secondly there is one of those spots that has that special "something". The unmade road comes to the riverbank and provides a restful scene. There are benches to sit on and just absorb the atmosphere. Immediately on my right there is a boathouse. Not just any boathouse though; this one has a thatched roof. It takes a marvelous photograph.

The pathway threads through a narrow alley taking me around Shillingford Court, and onward to Shillingford Bridge and back to the towpath. I look back towards the bridge and see the three stone arches. The bridge was built in 1827 and is another fine example of a river bridge. The positioning of this bridge is interesting, for it is exactly halfway between Reading and Oxford. It is a reminder of how far I have yet to travel, for Reading itself is still only halfway between the source and the flood barrier.

DAY SIX

SHILLINGFORD TO TILEHURST

17.6 Miles

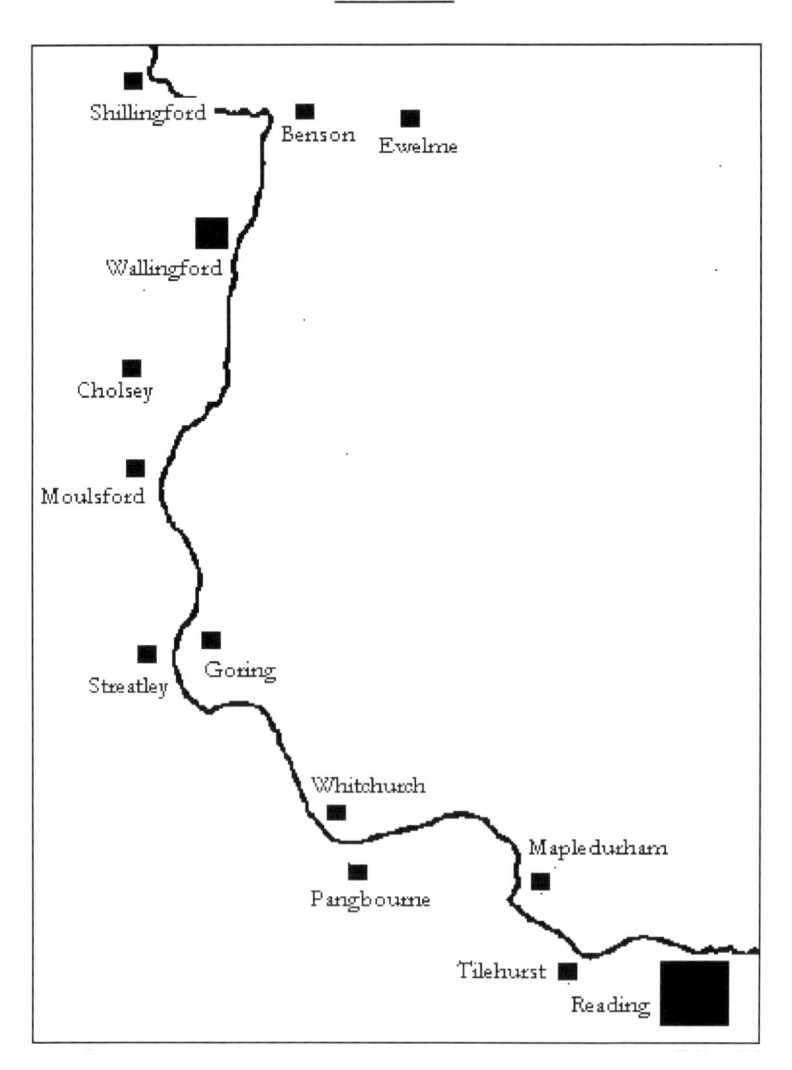

Jerome K Jerome

Although the river passes through Benson, it is the nearby village of Ewelme that holds an interest for anyone who has spent any period of time along the middle reaches of the Thames. The churchyard at Ewelme is the final resting place of Jerome K Jerome.

Jerome wrote "Three Men in a Boat" which was published in 1889 and the River Thames has not been the same since.

The book is fictional, although the main characters are based on Jerome himself (J) and two of his close friends, Carl Hentschel (Harris) and George Wingrave (George). Montmorency (the dog) was entirely fictional, although his mischievous nature was said to be more than a little bit based on the playful characteristics of Jerome himself.

Jerome started writing the book immediately after he returned from honeymoon with his new bride Georgina (more generally known as Ettie). It can be no coincidence that they spent their honeymoon along the banks of the Thames.

The book tells of the antics of the three friends on a trip up and down the Thames from Kingston to Oxford. Originally the book was meant to be a light-hearted travel guide for the newly popular pastime of boating on the river. During the writing Jerome's sense of fun gradually took over, and by the time the final version of the book was published it had become a humorous book in a travel setting.

Allegedly all of the inns and pubs mentioned in the book are still trading, which is a little fact that I have locked away in the memory-box. It seems to me to be a good opportunity for a pub crawl at some point in the future.

References to the book will keep cropping up during the walk, but it is the lives of the three men themselves that I am going to deal with here.

George Wingrave came into Jerome's life when the two of them rented rooms in the same house in Tavistock Place during JKJ's younger days and they became lifelong friends through a mutual love of the theatre. Wingrave worked in a bank, and eventually become manager of Barclays Bank in the Strand. He appears to have led a relatively quiet life, and his fictional adventures were probably much more exciting than his earthly existence.

Carl Hentschel was born in Lodz, Poland in 1864, and he migrated to England with his parents in 1869 at the age of five years. His father invented a photographic process which revolutionised the printing of illustration plates in books. The firm was very successful and Carl set up on his own and became even more successful. He too was a great theatre goer, and thus it was that he came into contact with Jerome and Wingrave. He was teetotal, which will come as a surprise to anyone who has read the book, for the character of Harris could be best described as a man who enjoyed a few bevies.

But it is Jerome himself who predictably provides the more interesting life history. He was born on May 2nd 1859 in Caldmore, near Walsall, Staffordshire. His father was Jerome Clapp Jerome and he was a somewhat unconventional character. Jerome Senior was originally a lay-preacher and part-time farmer, but had moved from Appledore to Staffordshire after a mining venture on his land turned sour and became an ironmonger. However he still maintained an interest in mining businesses and invested somewhat unwisely in them. The result was that the Jeromes became well acquainted with the local bailiffs and eventually lost all of their assets. The family moved to the Poplar area of London and relative poverty. His father died in 1871 when Jerome Junior was only twelve years old. At fourteen years of age young Jerome had little choice but to leave school to support his mother and sisters.

His first job was as a clerk with the London and North Western Railway at Euston. Following the death of his mother his sisters left home and he was free of all responsibility, he turned to the theatre. He assumed the stage name of Howard Crighton and toured the country as a jobbing actor, and we can assume this was not exactly successful. Disillusioned he tried journalism and writing, but all he was successful in was increasing his pile of rejection slips. He tried becoming a schoolmaster, where he appears to have enjoyed a similar success. Now totally demoralised, he tried a succession of dead-end jobs but remained firmly rooted to the bottom of the pile.

It was when Jerome was at his lowest that he had the inspiration that was to be the pivotal moment of his life. He decided to write a humorous account of his life as an actor. It was titled "On the Stage – and Off, the Short Career of a Would-be Actor" and was published in 1885. It is an absorbing account of life in the Victorian theatre, though its key to Jerome's future was that people found it very funny.

Spurred on by this success he wrote "The Idle Thoughts of an Idle Fellow" which was equally successful. He met and married Georgina Marris (Ettie) in 1888 and they went on their honeymoon along the Thames and the rest, as they say………….

The book was a runaway success. It reached sales of one million copies after just twelve years and is still in print. A mark of its popularity is that the year after the book was published the number of pleasure boats registered on the Thames leaped by fifty percent.

While Jerome is remembered mostly for his one work, he was a prolific and very successful writer of his day. He wrote twenty-one plays, ten novels, countless essays and was a prolific columnist. When the magazine "The Idler" was searching for a new editor, he beat Rudyard Kipling to the position. His literary friends included Kipling, J.M.Barrie, Thomas Hardy, Arthur Conan Doyle, H.G.Wells and Rider Haggard.

Jerome died of a stroke and brain haemorrhage on 14th June 1927. He is buried with his wife Ettie, her daughter from a previous marriage Elsie, and his sister Blandina by his side in the pretty churchyard of Ewelme, Oxfordshire, and a short walk from the banks of the river that made him famous.

Wallingford

Wallingford Bridge is a bit of a mongrel. The bridge was widened in 1809, and as a consequence the arches on the upstream side are rounded, while those on the downstream side are pointed. You can just imagine the construction company foreman saying "Just cover it with a bit of cement and we can all get down the pub for a swift half. No-one will ever notice."

The area has been strategically important since early times being the lowest place on the river that was fordable. So important did Alfred the Great consider it to be for the protection of Wessex that he built a fortified earthworks around the town much of which can still be seen today.

Wallingford was thought to be such a secure place that it had its own "Royal Mint". The mint was founded by King Athelstan sometime around 930AD and continued to supply silver coins for over three hundred years until the reign of Henry III.

In 1066 William the Conqueror crossed the river at Wallingford on his way to be crowned at London. William immediately recognised the strategic importance of this crossing and ordered a stone castle to be built to guard it. The castle was completed in 1071 and was of the typical Norman motte and bailey design. The Normans and their successors deemed this castle and surrounding area to be extremely important. The Domesday Book records that Wallingford was one of only eighteen towns in England with a population that exceeded two thousand. Wallingford was granted a Royal Charter in 1155 by Henry II, thirty two years before London received the equivalent accolade.

Wallingford boomed during the middle ages and was a major trading centre. The castle was a Royal Residence until the Black Death came calling in 1349. Plague killed many, and the town started to fall into decline. The final straw for Wallingford's fortunes was the construction of Abingdon Bridge in 1416 which had the effect of taking much of the town's trade away.

During the English Civil War Wallingford became a Royalist stronghold and held out against Cromwell's New Model army for sixteen weeks. The castle then became used by the Roundheads as a prison, but such was the risk that it could once again be used as a strong military centre against him if recaptured that Cromwell ordered it to be demolished stone by stone.

Wallingford has been peaceful ever since; peaceful that is apart from all of the murders. Dame Agatha Christie lived here and her fertile imagination gave fruit to the mystery stories beloved by so many. The queen of the "who dunnit" is still one of our best-selling authors and must have walked many times along these riverbanks.

Cholsey to Goring

After flowing through Wallingford the Thames enters another of its lonely stages. Crossing meadows and passing through the Cholsey Marsh Nature Reserve (today very aptly named because the rain was turning the path into a quagmire). The Chiltern Hills now provide the skyline across the river, gradually approaching the river until they come together a few miles further downstream at Goring.

To reach Goring I have to take a diversion through the village of Moulsford. The footpath leaves the river by a splendid example of one of Isambard Kingdom Brunel's fine brickwork railway bridges, and I gratefully squelch my way out of the marshy towpath and up to a well maintained path that circuits around Moulsford School and into the village.

You may have gathered by now that I do like to have the odd pint in the occasional hostelry. During my life I have spent more time than I probably should have within such establishments. However many I visit, I always find something different. So it is with a spring in my step that I turn down the lane leading me back to the river, for at the foot of the lane is something I know will be different. What would this next establishment hold for me?

How many sherberts do you have to have before you decide to call a pub "The Beetle and Wedge"? I have a mental image of the sign being a black insect crawling across a huge piece of cheddar but this is miles off the truth. The name derives from an old timber wharf that used to stand here. The "beetle" was the heavy mallet used to drive the "wedge" into logs, causing them to split so that they could be floated downstream.

H.G.Wells wrote "History of Mr Polly" while staying here, and the inn featured in the novel under the pseudonym of "The Potwell Inn".

Inevitably the inn is included by the ubiquitous Jerome in his classic tale as well.

It is worth mentioning at this point that while the surrounding views are changing as the Chilterns draw ever closer on the opposite bank, so the literature of the river is also changing. George, Harris, J (not forgetting Montmorency the dog) and their boat have been with me since Oxford and will remain with me all the way to Kingston, but Alice Liddel and her Wonderland adventures have been left well behind and I am stepping towards the idyllic homelands of Ratty and Mole.

The towpath is also changing. Since Cricklade there have been very few sections that benefited from the shelter of trees, and even these have been rather short (the sections that is, not the trees which have been normal tree-height). From hereon the tree cover will be much more frequent, making up the majority of the towpath's immediate vicinity until it too, in its turn, becomes replaced by the brick, stone and concrete of the capital city.

Goring and Streatley

The trees stop as suddenly as they started, and before me the white lock-house of Goring Lock provides a clear focal-point. It stands gleaming and demanding attention, perfectly framed by the surrounding hills. I have arrived at the Goring Gap.

On its journey to find the sea, the Thames came upon the Chiltern Hills and Berkshire Downs that combined to form a barrier to its progress. "Hmm", said the river, "I can't go over the top. On the other hand it is a long way round. Just have to bash my way through then". And so it did.

Geographers may not quite see it that way, but however it really happened over the course of ages, we are left today with the picturesque villages of Streatley and Goring nestling in the gap formed by the river flowing between the two sets of hills.

Streatley and Goring date back further than many first imagine. Here the inhabitants may sneer at references to the Domesday Book whence other places are proud to derive their earliest routes. There is evidence of a Neolithic settlement from the discovery of stone-age tools, and it is believed that this was an important crossing point for those very early residents of southern England. The ancient tracks of The Ridgeway and Icknield Way meet at the Goring side of the river and the travelers would have been able to make a crossing here if water levels permitted.

The Romans definitely had a presence here, for an old Roman milestone still stands at the Bull crossroads. The Bull public house, inevitably, was mentioned by "you-know-who", but there is a far more interesting part to the Bull's history. The garden is the burial place of a monk and a nun who were executed in 1440 for "misconduct". Whether the nun had been previously trained at Godstow Nunnery is not known.

The current bridge was completed in 1923 and replaced the original timber bridge built in 1837. Before this river crossings were by ferry. There are reports of a ferry disaster in 1674 when a ferryboat capsized in the flash lock and sixty passengers were drowned.

The towpath below Goring is narrow and muddy. I have to pick my way carefully along it because it has been made very slippery by the rains of the last few days.

After about a mile the Thames Path takes an inland detour to Whitchurch-on-Thames. The path climbs steeply, offering some superior views down to the river, and then sweeps into Hartslock Wood. This is typical Chilterns woodland, the path bobs up and down as it threads through the broadleaved trees, working its way around the hill, finally delivering me to a narrow lane that descends once more to the riverside and the charming village of Whitchurch-on-Thames.

Whitchurch and Pangbourne

In a way Whitchurch and Pangbourne are similar to Streatley and Goring. Both locations have villages on either side of a crossing.

Whitchurch Bridge is the second, and last, of the two toll bridges still operating on the river. It is owned by The Company of Proprietors of Whitchurch Bridge and was built in 1902. The company is empowered by Acts of Parliament to collect tolls at any time of day or night. There are plans to rebuild the bridge in 2013.

I stop and take some notes from the historic tariff poster on the side of the road. Pedestrians, sheep, pigs and boars were charged at 1/2d each, and carriages were rated at 2d for every wheel, a somewhat intriguing charge that must have had a good reason at the time. Modern day cars are charged at 20p, which includes all four wheels. Since decimalisation in 1971 pedestrians have been granted free passage, enabling me to cross the bridge with a clear conscience instead of trying to slip unnoticed around behind the back of the quaint toll-booth which is what I expect everybody tried to do before.

On the bridge there is a marvelous upstream view. The church spire provides a focal point above honey-coloured houses visible through a gap in the trees. The river runs alongside and reflects the buildings on its surface. I have a quiet bet with myself that those houses with their wonderful location will not be within the limits of my budget.

The Swan Inn at Pangbourne is a lovely establishment. It is situated right on the bank of the river, about as close as you could possibly get. The inn is 18th century, and is far larger on the inside than it first looks. A magnificent terrace provides a perfect setting for a well deserved lunch.

Once upon a time the Swan Inn sat exactly on the county boundary-line dividing Berkshire and Oxfordshire, and consequently each end of the bar was officially in a different county. These two counties had different licensing hours, and drinkers would move across the border for some extra drinking time when their own county called for last orders. No such problem existed for the regulars at the Swan. When the landlord called "Time Gentlemen please" they simply picked up their drinks and moved to the other end of the bar where they could continue to imbibe without the landlord getting his collar felt.

Finally, it was at the Swan Inn at Pangbourne that Jerome, George and Harris finally admitted that they had endured enough of rowing the River Thames. They looked at each other as they sat in the bar, said "Sod this for a game of soldiers" and went home.

The Wind in the Willows

Pangbourne is where the River Pang joins the Thames. Its most notable resident was Kenneth Grahame, author of "The Wind in the Willows". The sign for the village portrays the book to emphasise the connection. It is a little presumptuous of Pangbourne to claim Grahame as one of its favoured sons, because he only spent the last few years of his life here, and he had already found fame with his book before his arrival.

Kenneth Grahame was born in Edinburgh, but during his childhood he moved to live with his grandmother in Cookham, following the death of his mother. He attended St Edwards School in Oxford and wanted to go on to Oxford University. His grandmother had other ideas and sent him to work at the Bank of England. He worked diligently at the bank and his career developed well. By the time he retired due to ill health he had risen to become Secretary of the Bank of England.

Grahame had several stories published in various London periodicals, one of which, "The Reluctant Dragon", was turned into a film many years later by the Disney Corporation.

It was in 1908 that his most famous creation was published. "Wind in the Willows" tells the story of Ratty and Mole, who spent their days "messing about" on the river. Their lives are changed when they meet the conceited and wayward Mr Toad and they become swept up in many adventures as they attempt to save Mr Toad from himself.

The book made enough profits for Kenneth Grahame to retire, and he moved out of London to be near his beloved Thames, finally moving to Church Cottage at Pangbourne in 1924, where he lived out his final years until his death in 1932

Mapledurham

The river from Pangbourne follows a gentle curve across open fields to Mapledurham Lock, with Mapledurham House visible on the opposite bank.

Mapledurham House is one of several places that are considered to be the model for "Toad Hall". Although close to the river it is in fact very isolated with only a single road leading to the village.

The name "Mapledurham" is derived from "Maple tree enclosure" and is mentioned as two manors in the Domesday Book, Mapledurham Gurney and Mapledurham Chazey.

The house has been in the ownership of the descendants of the same family since Richard Blount purchased the estate in 1490. There was a slight interruption when the house was besieged and sacked by the Roundheads in 1643 and consequently sequestered by Parliament. The estate was returned to Walter Blount in 1651.

The estate has its own mill, unsurprisingly known as Mapledurham Mill. It is the only mill still working on the Thames and producing high-grade flour. There has been a mill here since before the Domesday Book, and the current structure dates from the 15th century. There have been many alterations and extensions since then to bring it to its current state.

Here is another one for the "not a lot of people know that" file. The mill was used for the cover of the eponymous album "Black Sabbath". Quite how the peaceful pastoral scene in front of me relates to a manic Ozzy Osbourne in full flow is hard to imagine.

The lock itself is in a wonderful setting and is a popular visitor destination. It holds the distinction of being the first power operated lock on the Thames, having electro-mechanical gear installed in 1955. A notice on the lock tells me that there are 78 miles to go to London, but does not detail exactly which bit of London.

The pathway takes another of its diversions from here, and I follow the footpath across the fields to Purley. It is another of those diversions caused by the awkwardness of a previous landowner. The towpath from Mapledurham Lock crosses over to the Oxfordshire bank for a mere half mile before crossing back again at Tilehurst. In the days of horse-drawn barges this would have led to a long delay as animals were ferried across and back again. My own inconvenience is relatively short for after a few minutes walking along the road a flight of steps by the boarded-up Roebuck public house takes me back down to the river.

I have reached a significant point on my journey. According to the various guides this is the exact halfway point. Ninety two miles completed; ninety two miles still to go.

DAY SEVEN

TILEHURST TO HENLEY

12.4 Miles

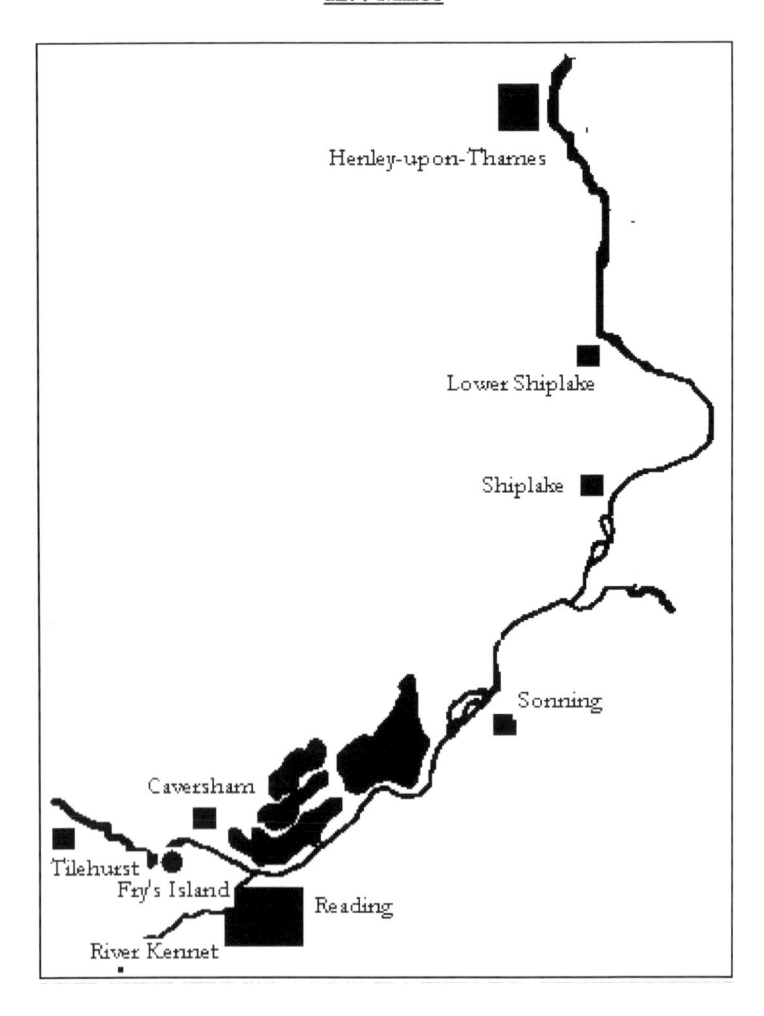

William Marshall

Caversham's most notable resident was William Marshall. "Who"? I hear you ask.

Marshall was the Mohammad Ali of his day. He was described as the "greatest knight who ever lived" and rose from a relative unknown to become one of the most powerful men in the land.

Born in 1146 William was the younger son of John Marshal, a minor nobleman. During his youth he was sent to Normandy to serve William de Tancarville and begin his training to become a knight. Training was hard, typically consisting of seven years of daily building up his strength and skills with both horses and weapons. The young William was a "natural" and soon discovered that he could make a good living by competing in tournaments.

Contrary to popular belief tournaments in those days were not relatively mild affairs with two knights on horseback poking lances at each other for the sake of a lady's handkerchief, but full bloodied staged battles where serious injury and even death were commonplace. Big money could be earned by capturing and ransoming opponents and there was no better practitioner than William Marshall. He was alleged to have competed in over 500 tournaments and was never captured.

Such was his success that Marshall became a medieval celebrity, and attracted much admiration. He soon caught the eye of King Henry II's son (also known as Henry) who was a keen tournament follower. In 1170 the Young Henry appointed Marshall as his personal tutor which further increased William's reputation. Marshall stood loyally by his employer through many difficulties during this period and his reputation continued to flourish. However in 1182 he was accused of "undue familiarity" with Margeurite of France who was married to Young Henry. As you can imagine this caused some friction with the King and William Marshall was banished from the Royal Court.

William Marshall continually petitioned the court of Henry II protesting his innocence and demanding trial by combat. Unsurprisingly there were no takers for this challenge and he continued to remain in exile from the court. However it was only a few months later when events took a sudden turn. Young Henry became terminally ill and summonsed Marshall to his deathbed. There Henry asked Marshall to fulfill his vow to go on a crusade. Marshall accepted and spent the next four years in the Holy Land completing the promise on Henry's behalf.

On his return Marshall was allowed to rejoin the court of Henry II and served his King through the many rebellions of the remaining three sons, Richard, Geoffrey and John.

When Henry II died the crown passed to his son Richard the Lionheart. After such a tumultuous period of rebellions the last thing the new King needed was a focus point for yet another dissenting voice, so he approached Marshall and invited him to join his court. This Marshall did, and served Richard with the same energy that he had given to his father.

Richard, in turn, showed his gratitude and in 1189 arranged for William to marry the most eligible heiress in the land, Isabelle de Clare. Isabelle was the daughter of the late Earl of Pembroke, and the title was awarded to William. In addition he was granted the estates of the former Earl, giving him large expanses of England, Wales and Normandy. The former penniless knight had finally arrived.

When John succeeded to the throne in 1199 William offered him his full support. However over the next few years they had some differences and Marshall spent several years on his estates in Ireland, diplomatically keeping out of the way. It was at this time that relations were becoming more strained between the King and the Barons, and it was to William Marshall that King John turned to for help and support over the issue of Magna Carta. So trusting was John towards Marshall that on his deathbed he appointed him to be protector to his nine year old son Henry III, and made him Regent of England to rule while his son was growing up.

Henry really needed the help of William Marshall. The disastrous reign of King John had left the Kingdom in chaos and there were minor rebellions everywhere. Marshall used his military skills and considerable diplomatic tact to keep the dissidents subdued. Marshall kept himself superbly fit, and at the remarkable age of 70 led the charge at the Battle of Lincoln against Prince Louis of France and some disaffected English noblemen. This battle saw the end of the various uprisings, and brought about the peace of 1217.

In 1219 Marshall knew that he was dying and he summonsed the barons and King to his castle at Caversham. The Bishop of Winchester was officially the King's guardian, but William did not trust him. Ignoring the Bishop's protestations Marshall entrusted the regency to the Papal Legate until Henry became of age.

His work done, William Marshall died on May 14th 1219. He was buried in the Temple Church in London, where his effigy can still be seen today.

Fry's Island

Fry's Island is also known as De Montfort Island following a famous duel on 8th April 1163 between Robert de Montfort and Henry Earl of Essex.

De Montfort had accused Essex of cowardice and treason. This followed a battle with the Welsh, where De Montfort alleged that Essex had dropped the Royal Standard and called out that the King was dead in an attempt to demoralise the English troops. Essex vigorously denied the charges and the two protagonists were always quarrelling. During the time that the Royal Court was in temporary residence at Reading, Henry II decided that he had suffered enough of the constant bickering and decreed that the dispute was to be settled by combat on the island in the middle of the Thames.

The duel was watched by thousands of spectators from the riverbank. No doubt that if they were around in those times Sky Sports would have given it some hyped-up title such as "Judgement Day" or "Fry's Fight Friday" or something equally banal.

Robert de Montfort was the victor, or in all probability this would now be known as Essex Island. The King ordered that Essex's body be transported to the local Abbey for burial. On arrival the monks discovered that Essex was not dead, but severely wounded. The monks tended to his injuries and in due time Essex achieved a recovery. However, because he had lost the combat he was considered to be guilty of his crime and was stripped of his lands. The King allowed Essex to live as a monk provided that he spent the rest of his days in exile at the Abbey.

Reading

The modern day railway traveler will inevitably, at some point, have to make a change at Reading Station. Much the same has taken place here throughout history. The town has been an important junction for all modes of transport. At first it was simply the river and the ancient roads, but later came the Kennet and Avon Canal that opened up the route to Bristol. This was followed by several turnpikes each providing faster travel between towns, and then came the railways and finally the M4 motorway.

There has been a settlement here since the eighth century when it was known as Readingum and the name is believed to derive from the Anglo Saxon for "Readdas People".

Reading Abbey was founded in 1121 by Henry I, who was later buried there. The abbey was situated at the confluence of the river Thames and River Kennet. During medieval times Reading Abbey was an important ecclesiastical centre and became one of the pilgrimage centres of England. During the peak of its fame it housed over 230 religious relics, including the hand of Saint James.

Reading became an important centre for the manufacture of cloth in the 16th century and became very wealthy as a consequence. The Civil War brought an end to all that prosperity with the town changing hands a number of times during the hostilities. Excessive taxes were levied on the town by both sides when they were in possession, and it was a long time before the Borough could recover.

Who can tell me the last time England was successfully invaded by foreign forces? The first answer many people will give is 1066, but some will point to Bonnie Prince Charlie who reached as far south as Derby in 1645. The correct answer is the "Glorious Revolution" of 1688, and the only significant fighting of that campaign was at the Battle of Reading on 9th December 1688.

James II had come to the throne in 1685, and immediately seemed to set his sights on becoming our most unpopular King. As we have already seen, there has been considerable competition for this title throughout our history. James' Catholic policy was certainly helping him on his way, and several of the "great and good" invited the Dutch William, who was married to James' daughter Mary to come and deliver England from the perceived tyranny of their King.

William landed at Torbay with his army on November 5th 1688, and marched through the West Country towards London to claim the crown. Such was the unpopularity of James that all opposition to the Dutch invaders melted away, and a conference was hastily arranged for James to meet William at Hungerford.

James had sent a detachment of troops to Reading as an advanced guard. By this time James had become so mistrusting of his people that these trusted guards were all Irish Catholics. The people of Reading did not like this at all, and feared that the royal guard would ransack the town and kill the inhabitants. They sent an urgent message to William to come at once to their rescue. William immediately responded by sending two hundred and fifty soldiers to Reading. Upon reaching the town their ranks were swollen by many of the local men, and together they drove the King's guard from the town. In the process the rebel forces suffered only five fatalities compared to fifty of the King's men.

William and Mary continued on their route to London, while James fled to exile in France. So it was that the "Glorious Revolution" returned England to Protestant rule and placed William and Mary on the throne.

Reading has also been strongly associated with the brewing industry. In particular the brewery founded in 1785 by William Blackwall Simonds. Simonds developed his business and in the process became the beer supplier to the army barracks at nearby Aldershot. He later expanded his operations to Malta and Gibraltar in order to keep those garrisons well watered. In 1830 the brewery exported bottled beer to the army in India, and India Pale Ale (IPA) came into being. The brewery was taken over by

Courage in 1960. The site of the original Simonds brewery is now occupied by the Oracle shopping centre.

Reading was also at one time the world's largest manufacturer of biscuits. For this we must go back to 1822 when the Crown Inn was a major coaching inn on the London to Bristol route. Opposite the Crown was a small bakery and confectioners owned by one Joseph Huntley. The coach passengers would visit his shop to purchase snacks for the journey. Huntley's most popular product was his biscuits, but they had an unfortunate habit of breaking during the bumpy journey. In one of those flashes of brilliance received by very few people, he started supplying his biscuits packaged in a protective tin. Not just any old tin, but a hand-painted tin of quality that people would want to keep and re-use. Hence Mr. Huntley cornered the market in biscuits. Later, in 1838 he went into partnership with George Palmer, who set up the distribution side of the business selling the products throughout the British Empire. At its peak in the early 1900's Huntley and Palmer employed over 5,000 people at its Reading factory. Sadly, the factory is now closed.

In common with Oxford, the Thames only touches Reading at the edges. Most of the borough sits on the River Kennet, and the next major feature is "Horseshoe Bridge" that takes the towpath over the mouth of the Kennet. This bridge takes the award for the worst bridge I have seen so far on my journey. It is a graffiti-strewn eyesore and is in complete contrast to the rest of the well-kept pathway through Reading. The only good thing about it is that it leads me into open meadows again for the walk downstream to the quaint village of Sonning.

Sonning

Sonning Lock is one of the prettiest and best kept locks along the River Thames. The lock house is adorned with colourful window boxes and containers of bright flowers are everywhere.

Very shortly after passing the lock I am off on one of my own small diversions. I turn right along a marked footpath and arrive at the beautiful flint-built church of St. Andrew. The church has been wondrously restored, and its walls stand out sharply from the surroundings. The churchyard is immaculately maintained, and each of the entrance gates to the church has a neat archway.

The village once possessed its own Bishop, the church being one of the cathedrals of the ancient Saxon diocese of Ramsbury and Sonning. It later became the home of the Bishop of Salisbury.

Conveniently adjacent to the church is the wonderful "Bull Inn" which boasts a very attractive courtyard and tabled terrace. The sun is by now well over the yardarm so it is time for a couple of refreshers and a sandwich.

The village itself is a very attractive place. Narrow streets are lined with well-maintained old houses and it is a delight to wind my way back to the river bridge to rejoin the pathway.

Sonning is a very ancient border village dating back to the earliest Saxon times. It used to mark the border between the ancient kingdoms of Wessex and Mercia, but now forms the dividing line between Berkshire and Oxfordshire. So specific is the boundary that there is a stone on the middle of the bridge marked with a vertical line to show the exact point where Berkshire changes to Oxfordshire.

The bridge is a beautiful multi-arched brick structure built in 1775. It is hump-backed in profile with the central arch being the largest, and the other arches tapering away on either side. The setting between the tree-lined banks is idyllic and has inspired many artists over the years to reproduce its beauty in many paintings and prints.

Sonning is the only bridge between Reading and Henley and consequently has a fairly heavy flow of traffic. There are traffic lights to control the vehicles, but pedestrians can cross over on the narrow footpath keeping tight to the wall.

Having spent some considerable time on the south bank of the river it is time to return to the north bank where I shall remain until Henley.

At the far end of the bridge there is an award-winning development. The old watermill has been completely renovated and converted into a theatre.

Three mills are recorded at Sonning in the Domesday Book, so milling had been a feature here for a considerable time. The Sonning mill expanded massively through the latter part of the nineteenth century and early twentieth century. However, even with all of the expansions to increase its output it eventually was no longer able to compete commercially with the massive new mill at Tilbury and it was closed down in 1969.

The mill remained empty for several years, and was then purchased by Tim and Eileen Richards in 1977. Together with Tim's brother Frank they converted the old mill into a dining theatre, which took them four years to complete. The mill now boasts an award-winning 215 seat air-conditioned theatre with a restaurant.

The towpath continues across more meadows until the high ground of Shiplake starts to grow ahead of me. The pathway passes in front of the Shiplake College boathouse and carries on to Shiplake Lock. Here the towpath takes another of its annoying trips to the opposite bank, and the Thames Path cuts inland through Lower Shiplake.

In order to return to the river, the pathway follows a track behind some more VNH's. Towards the end of the track one of the houses has a full miniature railway in its back garden, complete with its own little station. Unfortunately the owner is not playing with his pride and joy today so I continue onwards to the river, and a return to meadow land.

Henley

The ground underfoot changes suddenly from meadow to manicured grass. I have arrived at Henley-on-Thames. The sun is out and the riverside park is filled with afternoon activities. A short time to sit down and take in the atmosphere, and indulge in an ice cream from one of the convenient small cafes, and then I am off to the museum.

Screened by a row of trees from the towpath is a modern building dedicated to one of our oldest competitive sports. Henley is the home of English rowing, and the museum is dedicated to its history.

In the car park stands a pair of statues honouring the two most famous rowers these islands have produced. Sir Steve Redgrave and Matthew Pinsent are represented carrying their oars, walking towards the river for a hard days training session.

The main gallery is packed with rowing memorabilia, telling the stories of the history of rowing from the early Greeks, through the Oxford –

Cambridge Boat Race, the Henley Royal Regatta and finally to the great successes of the latest Olympic team.

There are also three other galleries well worth a visit. Next to the rowing gallery is an exhibition of the geography of the Thames, starting at the source and finishing at the estuary. Another gallery provides a pictorial history of the town of Henley-upon-Thames, but the final gallery is a delight of its own. Take the children to The Wind in the Willows. If you don't have children just go anyway and lose yourself in the world of Mr Toad and become a child one more. Press the audiophone to your ear and meander lazily among the models while the classical story unfolds about you. Meet Mr Toad with his caravan, see his car, stand before the judge and hear the jail sentence. Follow his escape cunningly disguised as a washerwoman and then cheer on Badger and his friends as they drive the dastardly weasels and stoats from Toad Hall. Finally stand and witness a triumphant and gloating Toad at the end.

Henley Bridge has a couple of interesting carvings on the centre of the Bridge. The bridge was designed in 1786 by William Hayward, but the carvings are by Mrs. Damer, who was a relative of Horace Walpole. The mask facing upstream is of Isis, and that facing downstream represents Tamesis, or Old Father Thames. Why Isis should appear at Henley, a long way downstream of Oxford is not known. It would make more sense, and resolve a lot of arguments if these heads were at Dorchester, but we have to enjoy them where they are.

The first ever boat race between Oxford and Cambridge took place at Henley on Wednesday June 10th 1829 at 8.10pm. Oxford were the winners, taking 14minutes and 30 seconds to row from Hambledon Lock upstream to Henley Bridge. Reports say that a crowd of 20,000 people turned up to watch.

It all started when two school friends from Harrow School went to the different Universities to continue their studies. Charles Merrivale, who was at Cambridge, sent a challenge to his friend Charles Wordsworth (nephew of the famous daffodil poet) at Oxford. Wordsworth accepted the challenge and thus the first boat race between crews from Oxford and Cambridge was arranged.

After suffering defeat Cambridge decided that Henley was not their lucky home, and the next time the challenge was issued the chosen venue was the Thames at Westminster, and the event has been staged in London ever since.

Several other races were contested regularly along the reach and attracted good crowds of spectators and supporters. All of these people required refreshment and accommodation that brought money into the town. The good residents of Henley knew a good thing when they saw one, and on 26th March 1839 a public meeting was held at the Town Hall and Henley Regatta was born.

The first event was held in 1839 and was so successful that two days were set aside for the following year. The regatta continued to grow in popularity, and in 1886 became a three day event, expanding into four days in 1906 and becoming the present five day extravaganza in 1986. Racing takes place from Wednesday to Sunday covering the first weekend in July.

Prince Albert attended the event in 1851 and ever since that day the regatta has enjoyed royal patronage and been known as Henley Royal Regatta.

The present rowing course is 1 mile and 550 yards (2,112m) long. All competitions are on a straight knock-out basis with the boats racing in pairs, one drawing the Berkshire bank and the other the Buckinghamshire bank. The main competition of the week is the Grand Challenge Cup which is awarded for men's eights. This cup has been competed for at every regatta since it was founded.

In 1908 and again in 1948 Henley was used for the rowing events at both of the previous Olympics that were held in London. All things must pass, and even the glory of Henley is now no match for the superb rowing facilities deemed to be essential for the modern Olympics. Some things don't change, however, and the new hosts of the Olympics are even more well-to-do than this upmarket town. The next Olympic venue will be the Eton College rowing lake at Dorney.

From Henley Bridge a distant object situated on the far bank has been constantly in view. Some unseen force seems to continually draw the eyes towards it, which was exactly the idea behind it. This is the Temple Folly, and was originally built in 1771 as a fishing lodge for the nearby Fawley Court. The Temple was designed by James Wyatt and the interior was inspired by the archaeological remains of ancient Pompeii in what is now known as the Etruscan style.

Temple Island was very conveniently situated for a starting point for the Henley Regatta, and it is from here that the races start. In Victorian times the Temple would be packed with revelers watching the regatta. Now it has been fully restored, and is available for functions. What an enchanting place for that special occasion.

DAY EIGHT

HENLEY TO MAIDENHEAD

16.3 Miles

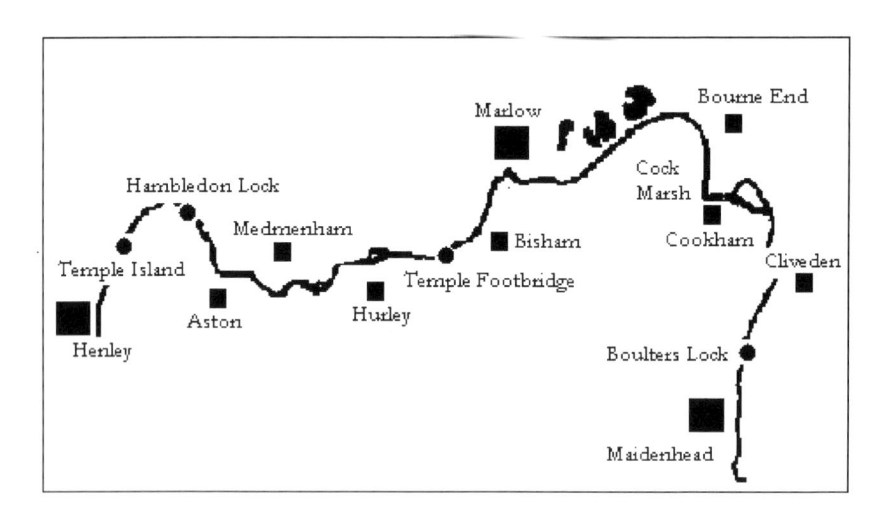

W.H.Smith

Beyond Temple Island the river starts to sweep to the right, turning two-thirds of a circle towards Hambledon Lock. Across on the far bank there is the beautiful Italian style mansion known as "Greenlands". This was built in 1853 for a certain William Henry Smith, who later became Viscount Hambledon.

"Ah yes", I hear you say, "Know him. He was the man who started up the newsagents". Not quite, for if it was named after the founder it would be H.W.Smith. Let me explain.

Henry Walton Smith and his wife Anna thought it would be a good business opportunity to start a small newsagents business. They opened a shop in Little Grosvenor Street, London and started to sell newspapers. Unfortunately Henry died after only a few months, and the business was continued by his widow.

The business thrived, and expanded into supplying stationery in addition to just newspapers. When Anna Smith passed away in 1816 the business was inherited by her two sons, Henry Edward and William Henry.

As in all things in life, there are seldom two equal parts, and the Smith brothers were no exception. William was by far the more competent businessman and in the way that these things evolve the business gradually became known as W H Smith.

The name changed again when William's son, also known as William Henry, reached the age of majority. He was made a partner in the company and it became known as W.H.Smith & Son in 1846.

The Smiths knew a business opportunity when they saw it. The railways were rapidly taking over the country, and they could see the future. The world and his wife would soon be standing around on station platforms waiting for yet another delayed train to make an appearance. How would people pass the time when they got bored? Answer; they would buy a book to read.

The first platform bookstall started trading at Euston Station on 1st November 1848. Then the Smiths opened a stall at another station, then another, and another.

Within a short period of time there were W.H.Smith bookstores everywhere across the network. To supply the stalls the Smiths developed their own distribution network with warehouses in Manchester, Birmingham, Liverpool and Dublin. W.H.Smith and Son soon became the number one book and newspaper distributors in the country.

So what do you do after you have achieved all that? Well, Smith Senior took retirement and Smith Junior decided to enter the world of politics. He was elected MP for Westminster in 1868, and in 1874 brought in a partner to the business, William Lethbridge, so that he could devote all of his energies to his political career.

In 1877 Smith was appointed First Lord of the Admiralty. Such an appointment to a man with no experience of the navy was somewhat controversial. Today we may expect our politicians to have no experience of life outside of being a Westminster "researcher" or professional politician, but in those days they expected rather more. Smith found himself the object of ridicule when Gilbert and Sullivan satirised him as the "Ruler of the Queen's Navy" in their comic opera "H.M.S.Pinafore". Indeed he allegedly became known as "Pinafore Smith" until the Liberals gained power at the next election and he found himself temporarily out of office.

The General Election of 1886 saw the Conservatives return to power, and Smiths political status grew. He was appointed Minister for War, then Leader of the House, and finally Warden of the Cinque Ports.

The business was handed down through two further generations of Smiths until mounting death duties became too much, and the family had no alternative than to sell shares in the business to the public. Over the years the family influence dwindled, and the last Smith to be on the board departed in 1996.

The rise and fall through so many generations. Three generations to build it all up, and then watch it slowly slip away. The house itself is now part of Henley Management College, so the business spirit started by Smith still continues to inhabit the grounds.

Hambledon and Aston

I follow the bend around and look at Hambledon Lock and Hambledon Mill. The mill can be reached by crossing the lock and then following the walkway along the top of the weir. Hambledon Mill is a popular subject for photographers with its large white walls and river frontage. I take a few snaps of my own, and then return over the lock to continue my walk towards Aston Ferry.

At Aston Ferry the traditional towpath takes another one of its trips to the opposite bank for a while. The Thames Pathway follows a narrow lane and climbs up to the hamlet of Aston, and The Flowerpot Hotel.

From the outside the hotel looks like one of those places that time has passed by. It probably looked exactly the same in Edwardian times. A large sign painted along the side-wall announces "Good Accommodation for Fishermen and Boaters". Walk inside and a wonderful Aladdin's Cave opens up. The walls are adorned with specimen fish set in glass cases and all sorts of other paraphernalia fill the gaps. It could take a few good drinking sessions to examine them all which is as good a reason as any for a return visit. Actually I will correct that. It is only a second good reason because the menu board is packed with mouth-watering dishes that have me positively drooling and making a note to come back in the future and bring the dearly beloved for a meal. (We returned in the autumn and it was well worth it).

The pathway turns off the narrow village road and runs parallel to the river, offering spectacular views down to the waterway and the fields beyond before heading back downhill to meet the river again.

Medmenham Abbey and the Hellfire Club

While the house I gazed upon some while earlier was a monument to the business acumen and entrepreneurial skills of the Smiths, the next estate, Medmenham Abbey, could not have a more different history.

The original Cistercian Abbey was founded in the 12th century and recognised by Royal Charter in 1200. It appears to have been a quiet place during its monastic existence (as these places were meant to be) until it was dissolved in 1547. It then passed through different family ownership until 1755, when all hell was let loose. To be precise "Hellfire" was let loose.

Medmenham Abbey became the headquarters of the notorious "Hellfire Club".

The club was founded in 1749 by Sir Francis Dashwood, and was one of many similar groups around the country. They attracted certain characters who we would mostly today refer to as "Hooray Henries" and enjoyed a reputation for drunkenness and debauchery. They were alleged to hold mock religious ceremonies and wear extravagant costumes and masks to conceal their identities when engaged in some of their more colourful proclivities. The exact activities of the club have never been established beyond the confines of rumour and vivid imagination.

Many of the Hellfire members were involved in politics and the membership allegedly included John Montague the Earl of Sandwich, William Hogarth, the Earl of Bute and the Prince of Wales. Benjamin Franklin was also a great friend of Dashwood and in all probability also took part in some of the sessions.

Eventually the Abbey became too notorious even for the Hellfire members, and Dashwood moved his club to the caves of West Wycombe that he had dug out for this very purpose. The caves are still there now, but I must push on and leave this den of iniquity behind.

Hurley

The pathway since rejoining the river has been mostly through woodland, but now I am back into open field and there are a lot more people about. This is partly due to the presence of a large caravan and camping park a short distance to my right, but also to the great popularity of this area for picnickers and families out for a walk. I am drawing nearer to the very popular area around Hurley Lock.

Hurley has had a settlement on the river since very early times. There is some documentary evidence of a ford being regularly used here as early as 450 AD. The village certainly existed in the days of the Danes, who called it Herlei. The Domesday Book of 1086 reports a Benedictine Monastery on the banks of the river.

The village is full of olde-worlde charm. The manor house, church and cottages all contributing their part, but the most striking feature is the great tithe barn with its flint walls stretching along the village street. Further along on the opposite side Ye Olde Bell is a real gem of a preserved building, just the way you imagine a very old pub should look like, and claims to have been standing since 1135. The parish church of St.Mary the Virgin was once the Priory Chapel.

The river here divides into a number of channels, forming seven islands in the river. These channels would have been very difficult to navigate, and boats would often be run aground on the shallows. An ideal place for a lock because mother nature has already carried out most of the digging by preparing suitable channels.

A wooden footbridge crosses over to the island on which the lock mechanisms stand, and a notice board displays the layout showing all of the islands. The lock island is frequented by many visitors during the summer months. The trees provide a welcome shade from the sun's rays, and there are plenty of bench seats and tables and chairs for the visitor to simply sit and watch the world go by. A refreshment hut is doing a steady trade and it is a great temptation not to be drawn towards it. When faced with such temptation there is only one thing that can be done; give in. So I bought an ice cream and sat down to watch life at the lock.

Temple

A rustic footbridge takes me back over from the island to resume the walk to Marlow. It does not seem that far before the towpath switches sides again. Until 1989 this particular crossing provided a major problem for walkers wanting to follow the river downstream. A ferry used to operate here but has been out of action since 1953 and walkers had to leave the riverbank and follow the road through Bisham in order to get to Marlow.

The problem was resolved in 1989 with the construction of Temple Footbridge which sweeps across the river to deliver the walker to the towpath on the north bank. At 150 feet across this is the longest wooden footbridge in Britain.

The area name is derived from the Knights Templar who owned Temple Mill Island, the mill and the surrounding lands. The mill once boasted the largest millwheel on the entire river, but it is no longer here. It was demolished to make way for the development of a marina towards the end of the 1970's. The mill had a complete working history until then. Originally built as a flour mill, it changed to a copper foundry in about 1710. This was made possible because the opening of the Thames and Severn Canal enabled copper to be carried by barge all the way from Swansea. The foundry then turned the copper into pots, pans and kettles in both copper and brass. In 1848 the manufacturing switched to brown paper and this continued until 1969 when the mill finally closed.

The Templars were also largely responsible for the next major building along the opposite bank, Bisham Abbey. There is evidence that the Templars occupied a building here from at least 1139. The building was considerably expanded around 1260. When the Templars were suppressed in 1307 the preceptory and its surrounding lands were confiscated by Edward II and granted to his various relatives. In 1310 the Priory was used as a place of imprisonment for Elizabeth Queen of Scots, the wife of Robert the Bruce. Elizabeth had been captured, along with her stepdaughter Princess Marjorie and sister-in-law Lady Christine of Carrick, during the Scottish Wars of Succession. All three were placed in custody under the direction of the King's Yeoman, John Bentley. They stayed at Bisham Abbey for two years before being transferred to Windsor Castle.

In 1335 the manor was purchased by William Montacute, the Earl of Salisbury, and it became the Salisbury family home for many years. Montacute founded Bisham Priory immediately next to the house, and the foundation stone was allegedly laid by Edward II. William Montacute was buried at the Abbey, as are several of his ancestors.

Another key figure from history is also buried here. Richard Neville, probably better known as "Warwick the Kingmaker" was also buried here in 1471 shortly after the Battle of Barnet.

The Priory was dissolved in July 1537, but only six months later was revived as a Benedictine Monastery by some monks who had been displaced from Chertsey. These monks were hopeful of being left in peace because they were dedicated to praying for the late queen, Jane Seymour. However, this was not to be, and they were forcibly evicted after only six months. When he was being dragged out of the chapel the Abbot, John Cordery, cursed the building, calling on God to witness that it should never be inherited by direct successors because some calamity would always befall the sons of those who later owned it. Nothing is now to be seen of the chapel or its associated monastic buildings.

The manor house was given to Henry's fourth wife, Anne of Cleeves, as part of her divorce settlement. Anne in turn exchanged the house with Philip Hoby for his house in Kent. The house remained in the Hoby family for many years.

The Abbey is now run by Sport England as a hotel, conference and training complex for elite sportsmen and women. Over twenty different sports regularly use the facilities, including the England football and rugby teams and individual sports such as tennis and judo.

All Saints' Church

Whilst the abbey has a fascination, one of the most striking views afforded by the Thames has been dominating the scenery for some time. As I have been walking along my eyes have been drawn to the wonderful edifice that is All Saints' Church. Pictures of the church alone do not do it justice. It needs to be seen in a much wider view to fully appreciate the effectiveness of a lone building standing right on the edge of the river. Everything about it looks just right.

The prominent feature is the Norman tower, dating from around 1175. It has a somewhat stumpy appearance, looking as though it should be a little taller to be in correct proportion to the rest of the building. This contributes to the unique shape of this church, helping to distinguish it from many others built at the same time.

The church has been expanded from its original size, mostly by the efforts of the Hoby family who took over the neighbouring Bisham Abbey from Anne of Cleeves. The several generations of the family left a very significant mark with a collection of monuments dedicated to their memory and a superb stained glass window displaying the heraldic arms of different branches of the family. The finest of the monuments was planned by Lady Elizabeth Holby (1528 – 1609) who was a bit of a live wire.

Lady Elizabeth Holby was an irrepressible woman. Her father was tutor to the young Edward VII and this enabled her to be married to Thomas Holby who was a wealthy translator and diplomat. Elizabeth was one of those women those of us who live in villages and small communities know well. If there something that needed to be organised she would do it, and God help anybody who tells her that they "do not have the time" to bake cakes, sell tickets or whatever else she demands that you do. She organised everything she could, from her daughters wedding to her own funeral. Elizabeth loved to show off her organizational prowess at court, and especially loved to "put one over" Lord Burghley at every opportunity. Apart from the fine family memorial Lady Holby's high point was persuading Queen Elizabeth I to hold her court at Bisham Abbey for a six week period in 1592. You can just imagine her ladyship punching a clenched fist into the air with a defiant shout of "Yes! Beat that Burghley!"

We all know you just can't get rid of people like Elizabeth Hoby, and she is no exception. I say "is", rather than "was", because she allegedly still walks the corridors of Bisham Abbey taking charge of the place. This is probably why Bisham is so popular as a retreat for leading football clubs. The thought of running into Lady Hoby on one of her missions would frighten the most party-loving Premiership prima-donna into instant docility.

The Holby family was responsible for much of the expansion to the church but the final touches were the result of extensive restoration work that commenced in 1849. A new vicar, Rev Thomas Powell had arrived and set about developing All Saints into its present glory. He was to stay at All Saints for over fifty years. Powell enlisted the financial patronage of the Vansittart family who were now the owners of Bisham Abbey. The chancel was extended and the south gallery constructed. The Vansittart's were an unfortunate family, with several young heirs dying in tragic circumstances. Was this the curse of Abbot Corderey? There is a memorial in the church to one of the sons who died while at Eton.

The final addition was made in 1878 by General Owen Williams who built the north aisle in memory of his parents and first wife. This gives the fine building that sits across the water from me now, its stone features reflecting in the slow-moving waters of the River Thames.

Marlow

Moving along the river starts to bend, and the curve gradually reveals one of the classic Thames views, the spire of All Saints Church and the fine outline of the suspension bridge stretching across the water.

The bridge was designed by William Tierney Clark (1783 – 1852) and opened in 1832. There had been a bridge across the river at Marlow since the days of Edward III. The need for the new bridge was that the old wooden bridge had proved insufficient and had collapsed in 1828.

William Tierney Clarke had studied under the supervision of two of England's greatest civil engineers, Thomas Telford and John Rennie. Such was the effect of his new bridge across the Thames that in 1838 he was asked to design a similar bridge (the Szechenyi Chain Bridge) to cross the River Danube and link the two cities of Buda and Pest to form Budapest. This was to be a much longer bridge, nearly three times the size of its smaller prototype. When completed it had a span of 660 feet and at the time was the longest bridge in the world. There are commemorative plaques on both bridges marking the connection between them. Neither bridge today is the original. The Szechenyi Bridge had to be rebuilt after it suffered wartime damage, and in 1965 Buckinghamshire County Council restored the Marlow Bridge replacing the original ironwork with steel.

On the opposite side of the river is the Compleat Angler Hotel, one of the most famous on the Thames. It is named after the book written by Izaak Walton (1593 – 1683) and first published in 1653. This hotel is frequented by the rich and famous, and offers superb cuisine and accommodation. One of the hotels claims to fame is that in 1999 it became the first public restaurant outside of London to be visited by The Queen for a meal. This gives it more than a little "one-upmanship" on all of the other hotels who can merely claim that Jerome K Jerome mentions them in "Three Men in a Boat".

For a small size town Marlow has had more than its fair share of notable residents. A memorial in the porch of All Saints Church commemorates Sir Miles Hobart, who was instrumental in starting one of our more quaint Parliamentary traditions. Hobart began the practice of Black Rod having the door of the House slammed in his face. He was Member of Parliament for Marlow and became famous when he locked the door to Parliament and refused entry to the Kings Messenger during a debate. For this little escapade he was imprisoned in the Tower of London. Shortly after his release he was killed in an accident when the horses on his carriage bolted on Holborn Hill. This monument was paid for at public expense by Parliament and is the first example of a public memorial in England.

The poet Percy Shelley also lived in Marlow for a while and a plaque on the wall of Albion House in West Street commemorates this. He wrote "The Revolt of Islam", one of his major works, while at Marlow. The title is somewhat misleading in this present age because it has very little to do with Islam as we would know it today. The plot of the poem is that the leading two characters, Laon and Cyntha stage a bloodless coup against the Sultan of the Ottoman Empire. At the same time Mary Shelley, Percy's wife, wrote her most famous novel "Frankenstein".

The Shelley's great friend and literary colleague, Thomas Love Peacock, also lived in West Street, at number 67. There must have been something very literary in the air in West Street because a century later the writer T.S.Elliot (1888 – 1965) moved into number 31 and stayed for two years at the end of the First World War.

The attractiveness of Marlow with its charming riverside landscape coupled with close proximity to London makes it a very attractive place to live, and celebrities abound. How fitting then, that Marlow's most celebrated current resident should be one whose success in life is due to all of his work on the river. Sir Steven Redgrave, five times Olympic champion is celebrated with a bronze statue in Higginson Park, just upstream of the bridge. He is looking across the river at the finishing post for the annual Marlow regatta.

From Marlow Bridge the Thames Pathway takes another of its excursions. From the bridge to the lock there is no footpath, and in times gone by the horses would have to be unharnessed and walked to the downstream end of the lock, while the barges were hauled by long ropes through the lock. The path is known as "Seven Corner Alley", but I reckon the man who named it lost count somewhere. The pathway goes up the side of the bridge, over the road, up the street, cuts through the churchyard, over another street, round "The Two Brewers" pub, then twists and turns until I find myself back at the riverside.

Bourne End and Cock Marsh

After Marlow the pathway leads me under the bypass bridge and out into open countryside again. On the opposite bank the steep wooded banks of Quarry Wood cut across the line of the river, which turns sharply to the left to continue on its way. A broad track opens up and it is very quick easy walking across the meadows towards Bourne End.

Bourne End takes its name from Burnend, meaning the end of the stream, and it is here that the river Wye joins the Thames. This area is hugely popular with the boating fraternity, and a large marina runs alongside the pathway. More correctly I suppose the pathway really runs through the marina. The area is also home to the Upper Thames Sailing Club which has been here since 1884. There are boats everywhere, and this being a Sunday there are plenty of youngsters out in dinghies as well. There really are an enormous amount of boats here. I sit and watch all the action for a while, and then leave for the quiet of Cock Marsh

Cock Marsh is owned by the National Trust and is on the opposite bank, which I reach by crossing over the Bourne End Railway Bridge. The marsh is a lowland reserve supporting redwing, lapwing and wading birds. The reserve covers 130 acres and also includes some bronze-age burial mounds. My path follows the riverside edge of the reserve then moves into open meadowland again as the village of Cookham comes into view.

The pathway leaves the river and diverts through the delightful village of Cookham. I enter the village through the churchyard and look back on the picturesque Holy Trinity church that is very popular as a wedding venue. As nice as it is this is not the church that I have come into Cookham to see, it is a far smaller and more modest building that is of interest and it is a few hundred yards further on around the corner.

Sir Stanley Spencer

I finally arrive at my destination, a small former Methodist Chapel. This is the home of the Stanley Spencer Gallery, dedicated to preserving the memory of one of Cookham's most famous residents, Sir Stanley Spencer.

Spencer was one of England's better known painters. His work is quite remarkable. He had a great love of his home village and he was also a very religious man. So he put the two together and composed vivid pictures of Biblical tales, but set them in his beloved Cookham.

Stanley Spencer was born on 30th June 1891, the eighth child of Annie and William Spencer.

In 1908 the young Stanley studied at the Slade School of Fine Art at the University College of London. Not for him was the typical student life, for he spent most of his spare time commuting back and forth to Cookham, so much so that he soon earned the nickname "Cookham" from his fellow students.

In 1914 he began military service in the Royal Army Medical Corps, and in 1916 was sent to Greece.

Spencer was a war artist during WW2, and his most celebrated pictures at the time depicted the shipbuilding industry on the banks of the Clyde.

In 1925 he married Hilda Carline who was also an artist. They initially set up home in Hampstead and moved to Burghclere in 1927. He just could not stay away, and returned to Cookham in 1932 where he stayed until he died.

In 1927 Spencer held his first one man exhibition in London. His painting "Resurrection Cookham" was highly acclaimed. The painting can currently be seen in the Tate Gallery, and shows the residents of Cookham rising from their graves in Cookham Churchyard.

Spencer was a popular figure in Cookham. He would often be found at work, or pushing a battered old pram in which he carried his easel, canvasses and paints. He was a very sociable person, and was known to be able to talk for hours as his mind explored his wilder imagination.

Stanley Spencer received his knighthood in 1959, and died later that year.

The gallery was opened in 1962, three years after his death. It is run by volunteers and holds over 100 paintings and drawings. In 2007 the chapel was completely renovated with a grant from the Heritage Lottery Fund, transforming the old chapel into a modern light gallery of his work. The centre-piece is his unfinished work "Christ Preaching at Cookham Regatta" which I found was best viewed from the upstairs balcony. The work depicts Christ in the centre, preaching to a boatload of Cookham parishioners while the regatta goes on around them.

Before leaving Cookham, there are a couple of connections with Wind in the Willows that are worthy of mention. Kenneth Grahame spent his childhood years here at "The Mount" in Cookham Dean. The nearby Quarry Wood is thought to be the inspiration for the "Wild Wood" in his masterpiece. Much more interesting is that Lullebrook Manor in Ferry Lane could be his inspiration for Toad Hall. Particularly when you consider that the owner at the time was the first person in the area to own a motor car and liked to show off his pride and joy. It could be just a coincidence, but let us not let an absence of proof get in the way of an entertaining story.

Cliveden

The pathway does not return immediately to the river, but takes a necessary diversion and I will rejoin the main river a little downstream of Formosa Island. The reason for the deviation is that the river suddenly splits into four channels creating much chaos for the earlier barge owners. A system of four ferries was required to get all of the horses and barges through these natural obstacles and the Thames path takes a much more realistic route across the fields. The route twists around the field boundaries and suddenly comes to a sudden stop at the remains of an old ferry landing stage. I am back at the waterside at Old Lady Ferry with a steep wooded hillside on the opposite bank. This is spring and everything is freshly painted green, but in the autumn it is a cascade of yellows and browns. A convenient wooden bench allows me to sit and look at the banks opposite. Through the gaps in the trees can be seen well-tended gardens and cottages. I am back in notoriety land, for this is the Cliveden Estate.

The plateau on the opposite hill is a wonderful location for a home. George Villiers, the 2nd Duke of Buckingham certainly thought so and began to build the first house here in 1666. From 1739 to 1751 it was let to the Price of Wales, and it was here that the song "Rule Britannia" was first performed at a theatre party held in the gardens. In 1795 the house was severely damaged in a fire and was not restored for another 30 years. Within a few years this, too, was destroyed in a fire and the house was totally rebuilt in 1851.

The current house was designed in Italian style by the architect Charles Barry for the 3rd Duke of Sutherland. The three-storey mansion passed through several hands, with each owner making modifications to the internal design and adding their own follies and statues to the gardens. Eventually the property was purchased in 1893 by the Astor family and in 1919 began its journey to infamy when it became the home of Waldorf Astor and his wife Nancy. This couple were the "fabulous Astors" and the house became known for its lavish parties for the rich and well-connected. His wife, Nancy Astor became the first woman Member of Parliament to take her seat in the House of Commons. She was not, as is commonly but mistakenly assumed, the first female to be elected to Parliament. That honour belongs to Constance Markiewicz. Constance was a firebrand of her day and was a prominent figure in the fight for Irish Nationalism. She was elected to Parliament in 1918 as a Sinn Fein representative for Dublin St Patrick's constituency. In line with Sinn Fein policy she refused to take her seat in Parliament and so the first woman to sit on the benches was Nancy Astor.

Waldorf Astor gave the Cliveden Estate to the National Trust in 1942 on the condition that the family could continue to live in it.

It was in the early 1960's that all the partying of the Astors paled into insignificance with the public scandal that became known as "The Profumo Affair".

Osteopath to the famous and London playboy, Stephen Ward organised a party at Cliveden that was attended by Christine Keeler who was described at the time as a "showgirl". At the party Keeler met the current Minister of War, John Profumo and they embarked on a brief affair. At the same time Keeler was conducting another "affair" with Russian naval attaché Yevgeny Ivanov who was based at the Russian Embassy. With the cold war at its height alarm bells should have been ringing all over the place, but everything stayed quiet until a year later when everything went up at once.

Profumo was questioned about the affair in the Commons, and emphatically denied everything and threatened to sue any accuser who dared take it further. He thus broke two unwritten rules, number one don't get caught, and rule number two when in a deep hole stop digging. The press had the inevitable field-day and Profumo was forced to resign.

The scandal severely damaged the public confidence in Harold MacMillan's Government and this took its toll on the Prime Minister, and he too resigned a few months later suffering from ill health.

The estate is still owned by the National Trust but the house is now a lavish hotel. It is open to the public and you can walk through the same enchanting woodlands and enjoy the same gardens and spectacular views over the Thames as did those high-society party-goers of the Astors. Just don't talk to any showgirls or Cabinet Ministers.

Boulter's Lock

It is a pleasant walk along the river to Boulter's Lock. The towpath is narrow and right up against the flowing waters. A canopy of trees provides shade from the afternoon sun and the far bank provides a wall of greenery interspersed with the occasional cottage.

The small bridge at Boulter's Lock provides access to Ray Mill Island. This is a delightful little diversion, if only to take advantage of the ice cream kiosk. A notice on the island informs me that a walk around the perimeter will take about 1000 steps, and be a tenth of my daily requirements to maintain and improve my fitness. Seeing as I am doing a minimum 30,000 steps a day without these diversions I don't think this will be over-stretching things, so off I go.

Cornetto in hand I spend some time at the aviaries, with their selection of birds, before sitting by the weir for a while.

The island takes its name from the Ray family who had a mill here in the 18th century.

The weir at the top of the island has a flume created for canoeists, and is also the site of a salmon ladder. In fact all of the weirs from Teddington upstream to Mapledurham have salmon ladders as part of the Thames Salmon Rehabilitation Scheme.

The scheme was started in 1979 with a target of returning naturally breeding salmon to the Thames system. The salmon cycle runs like this. The salmon spawn in upper freshwater tributaries, such as the Kennet. The eggs hatch and the first young, known as alevins, are introduced to the world. As they grow they are called parr, and after two years reach the stage known as smolt, when they attain a silvery colouring. When the smolt reach this stage they start on their long journey downstream to the sea. Once they are in to the open sea they rapidly put on weight, and in one to three years nature urges them to return to the river and begin the cycle all over again.

It seems to have been very successful in the early years, with ever-increasing numbers returning to the river from 1982 to a record year of 2003 when 338 fish were recorded. Since then numbers have rapidly declined again, and no fish were recorded in 2005, and only two in 2006.

The problem seems to be related to the condition of the river during the peak salmon run months of July and August. Low rainfall means that the flow levels are insufficient to entice the fish upstream. If you add higher than normal water temperatures the capacity of the water to hold enough oxygen becomes a further deterrent. The last two summers have seen heavy rain and this is just as bad for the fish. The swollen stormwaters carry extra silt and contaminants that the salmon see as a sort of chemical barrier, and again they are deterred from their journey.

In an attempt to regenerate the programme some 40,000 salmon smolts have been released into the River Kennet. These worked their way downstream to the sea, and it is hoped that survivors from their time in the sea will return to the Kennet to breed.

Maidenhead

Retracing my steps back to the Pathway, I pause to take a photograph of the covered wooden footbridge across the sidestream before crossing the main footbridge. I notice a blue plate on the bridge, informing me that the broadcaster David Dimbleby once lived in the adjacent house.

Today is rather quiet along the pathway, but this was far from the norm in Victorian and Edwardian times. The area around Boulters Lock down to the Maidenhead Bridge was the "Thames Riviera", particularly on the weekend after Ascot Week. This was where the well-to-do would hold their boating parties and promenade their ladies up and down the riverside, while the lower classes flocked there to watch the toffs. A sort of real-life "Hello!" magazine of the time. The scene can be viewed today in the painting by Edward John Gregory (1850-1909) "Boulter's Lock, Sunday Afternoon" that is on display in the Lady Lever Art Gallery, Port Sunlight, Merseyside.

Maidenhead reveled in its popularity, and the town became prosperous on the back of this tourist trade. All came to a sudden stop with the events of 1914, and the revelry has not taken place since.

It is a pleasant walk along the old promenade to Maidenhead Bridge. The pathway is only separated from the river by an iron railing, and an avenue of trees forms a barrier between me and the road. About halfway between the block and the bridge is an engraved slab in the pavement bearing the ode;

> *Old Father Thames goes gliding by*
>
> *As ripples run he winks his eye*
>
> *At Cotswold cows & Oxford dons*
>
> *Nodding to Windsor's royal swans*
>
> *He bears our nation's liquid crown*
>
> *By lock & weir to London town*
>
> *May all that know and love his banks*
>
> *Pause here awhile to offer thanks.*
>
> *2002*   *Ian Miles*

So I offer thanks and move on.

Maidenhead is a relatively new development compared to many of the places I have already visited on this walk. Neighbouring Bray and Cookham are far older and it seems as though Maidenhead was just conveniently dropped into the middle to fill a gap. This settlement was originally named South Ellington, and it was here that a wooden bridge was constructed around the mid 13th century following an order from Henry III for the road to be widened. This made the areas fortune, because now the town was on the main highway between London and Bath, and luckily for South Ellington exactly a one day coach journey from London, making it the ideal stop-over point. With the stop-over there came the rush of tradesmen to service the travelers, not only the obvious coaching inns, but also stables, blacksmiths, coach repairers and all the support services required to maintain the transport system. The town grew rapidly.

Soon a new wharf was built near to the bridge to cope with deliveries of goods. In the language of the time "New Wharf" was "Maiden Hythe" which soon became corrupted to Maidenhead and the name has stuck ever since.

With such a transport centre already in existence it was inevitable that this was a natural place for the new railway and the Great Western Railway came to town in 1838. People soon realised that Maidenhead was close enough for the better paid populace to travel by train to London each day and return again in the evening. The commuter was born. The area also developed a scandalous reputation for the growing number of fun-seekers and playboys who came out of London seeking their pleasures.

I too am seeking out the station to return home for the evening. The station itself is a drab affair not at all in keeping with its previous high status, but on the way to it there is a small bonus and the possibility of earning a quick pint in a pub bet. My chosen route takes me along York Road, past the home of Maidenhead United Football Club. Allegedly this is the oldest continually used football ground in the world. I tuck this snippet of information away in the hope of running into one of my pub quiz friends (who is probably the leading authority on English football grounds having personally visited them all from the heights of the Premiership down to the bare grass-roots of the lower Unibond), to see if he knew this obscure fact. Sadly he did.

DAY NINE

MAIDENHEAD TO SHEPPERTON

20.4 Miles

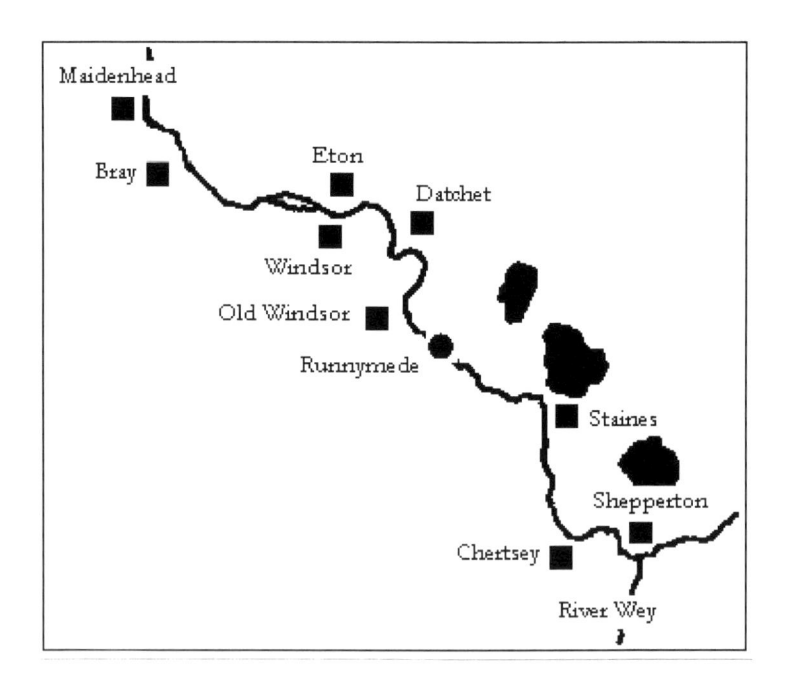

Maidenhead Railway Bridge

Maidenhead Road Bridge is a fine example of eighteenth century design and workmanship. A series of thirteen arches support the busy A4 roadway which in turn is protected at the sides by a decorative balustrade. Fine example though it is, as a feat of engineering it is dwarfed by the next bridge, the Maidenhead Railway Bridge.

Maidenhead Railway Bridge (or Maidenhead Viaduct) was designed by the great Isambard Kingdom Brunel, and is considered to be the best of the three bridges that he constructed over the Thames. (The other two I have already passed being situated back upstream at Gatehampton and Moulsford).

The construction is all brick, and provides a colourful photograph standing out in deep red against the background grey skies. Just two great arches support the tracks, and at the time it was built these were the widest bridge arches in the world at 128 feet (39m) each. These were also the flattest arches with a rise of only 24 feet (7m). This was essential if Brunel was to retain his obsession with keeping to long and gentle gradients on his railway. So successful was he at achieving this target that the gradient on this whole stretch around Maidenhead has a slope of only 1 in 1,320 a remarkable piece of civil engineering.

Not everyone was confident that Brunel's engineering would prove to be as effective as he claimed. The board of the Great Western Railway had a touch of the "health and safety" panic and ordered that the wooden framework used to support the arches during construction should remain in place as additional insurance against the bridge collapsing under the weight of the trains. Good old Isambard was having none of it, and arranged for the supports to be slightly lowered so that everything still looked hunky-dory to the men with the clipboards but in fact the support was non-existent. Some years later those wooden supports (or more correctly non-supports) were washed away in floods and the men in suits were astonished when the bridge did not fall down. Brunel was able to say "Told you so" and the framework was never replaced. One can imagine that Brunel is up there somewhere, perched on a cloud with his harp, looking down and saying to the former railway board members, "180 years and still going strong; stick that in your waistcoat pocket".

The bridge was famously painted by J.M.W.Turner (1775-1851) in his 1844 painting "Rain, Steam and Speed – The Great Western Railway" that can be viewed in the National Gallery, London.

According to the guidebook the arch under which the Thames Pathway passes is known as the "Sounding Arch" because it has a spectacular echo. So as I walk underneath I give a shout (it has to be done) to see if it is true. It is.

Oakley Court

There is something familiar about Oakley Court, a mock Gothic castle-like building on the opposite bank. I have never walked this stretch before but I have definitely seen that building somewhere before.

It was built in 1859 for Sir Richard Hall Say, and there is a story that he wanted it constructed in the style of an old French Chateau to stop his young French wife from being homesick. What a lovely thought, who said romance was dead? Except that his wife was Ellen Evans from Boveney which is just along the road! As I am often known to say, let us not let the facts get in the way of a good story.

After several different owners the house was bought in 1919 by Earnest Oliver, who was a somewhat eccentric character. He often entertained foreign diplomats and would fly their national flags as an expression of courtesy while they were staying with him. During the war there are rumours that Oakley Court was the England headquarters of the French Resistance, and that General De Gaulle was a frequent visitor.

Mr. Oliver passed away in 1965 and the house lay uninhabited for several years. It was during this time that it was used for the purpose that had sparked something deep in my own memory.

In 1955 the film company Bray Studios moved to Down Place, immediately next door to Oakley Court. When their neighbouring property became vacant it provided an immediately accessible location for filming, and so it became St.Trinians School for Young Ladies, the setting for The Rocky Horror Show, Dracula's Castle and the backdrop for umpteen reels of spooky house footage from Hammer Films.

Oakley Court was converted into a hotel, and has been open since 1981. It is apparently a popular destination for Rocky Horror Show fans, so if you want to book in and do the "Time Warp" in the true location you will very possibly find that you are not the only one.

Boveney

Approaching Boveney Lock I was surprised to find a small church sitting in splendid isolation just a few yards from the towpath. The walls are made of chalk rubble, and garrotted with small flints pressed into the mortar. There is a wooden bell-tower that houses three bells.

This is the church of St Mary Magdelene and it once served the village of Boveney which lays a few hundred yards away from the river. The church is undoubtedly old, being known to have been in existence from before 1266 when it was part of the Parish of Burnham.

In times gone by this stretch of the Thames at Boveney was used for the loading of timbers from the Windsor Forest on to the Thames barges. This would have entailed a large workforce at the wharves, and the church would have served a large number of wharf workers and bargees in those days. The area has been much quieter over the last part of the twentieth century and the church gradually fell into disuse.

St Mary Magdalene was declared redundant in 1975, but local campaigning for its preservation resulted in the building being leased to a society known as "The Friends of Friendless Churches", who are currently undertaking some restoration work on the church. The church is still a consecrated building although services are only held three times per year.

Naturally our friends just up the river at Bray Studies simply could not resist the allure of this place, and it has featured in several of their "Hammer House of Horrors" films.

Seats have been thoughtfully provided along this part of the riverbank making it a very peaceful place. There is a car park close by so it is inevitably also very popular.

Eton

There have been several periods in my life where I have found myself involved in fundraising for building new facilities for local schools. These have included swimming pools, computer facilities and a modern art facility. Inevitably this involves organising car-boot sales, "Merry Christmas" raffles and family BBQs, with each one adding a further few quid to the coffers and eventually the target is reached. It is always a grind, often seeming so much work to gain every little step closer to the objective. So just imagine your reaction if someone stood up at your next PTA meeting and says that it is about time that your school had its own International Sports Arena to hold World Championships and a future Olympic Games.

It is probably a lot easier if the school happens to be Eton College, but even then it is still a remarkable achievement. The 2000m rowing course has its own modern designed boathouse and was the host for the 2006 World Rowing Championships. The next major event will be the 2012 Olympic Games. It is certainly a huge piece of "one-upmanship" on all of the other rowing clubs I have passed so far.

I am now approaching Windsor and people are starting to appear along the pathway and in the fields. I do not know it yet, but I have just completed all of the lonely stretches. From now on there will be people around most of the time.

The bank opposite Windsor Racecourse is known as "Athens". This was a favourite bathing spot for the boys of Eton College. The school rules demanded that "boys who were undressed must either immediately get into the water or get behind screens when boats containing ladies come in sight". These days it would probably become a major attraction for ladies.

Windsor Castle is standing proudly on its hill, and after one more meadow I arrive at the narrow streets of Eton. After two turns in the road I am at Windsor Bridge, looking straight across the river at the largest inhabited castle in the world.

There has been a bridge here for over 800 years. The present bridge has been standing since 1822. Like many other bridges on the Thames the charging of tolls became very contentious and tolls were stopped in 1897 after many legal disputes. Road traffic was banned from 1970, and because of this I can now sit on the seats provided on the bridge and take in the view of the magnificent castle.

The bridge was also a boundary point for the boys of Eton College. Until 1990 they were not allowed to cross the bridge into Windsor unless they were wearing a jacket and tie. This must have caused much merriment among the locals. Who could have resisted shouting out "Oi! Lordship! You can't come over here without a jacket and tie"

Windsor

Windsor marks the start of the Royal Thames. Our Royals throughout the ages have preferred to live away from the city. In earlier times this was primarily to avoid the diseases and smells of the capital, although the facilities for hunting in the countryside no doubt also played a considerable part. It was the River Thames that provided their escape route from London.

Moving about in those days involved transporting a huge retinue of household staff, courtiers, musicians and assorted hangers-on and it was far easier and a lot more comfortable to transport everyone by river. Windsor was as far upstream as they ventured, and seems to have been the most popular. The pathway will take me past other Royal Palaces of Hampton Court, Richmond and Kew, but here, directly in front of me, perched defiantly on its hill and imposing its authority across all it surveys is the magnificent Windsor Castle.

Windsor Castle is one of the oldest and largest inhabited castles in the world. It has stood here for over 900 years. The edifice before me is the result of our rulers through the ages "getting the builders in" to add their own particular legacy.

William the Conqueror was the first to recognise the current site. Edward the Confessor had a castle three miles downstream at what was then known as Windsor, but William built his castle in what was then the manor of Clewer. The castle was known as Windsor Castle and appears with that name in the Domesday Book. Later the two settlements were renamed Old Windsor and New Windsor but the "New" tag fell out of use and it simply became Windsor.

The original castle was built of wood, and was the typical Norman "Motte and Bailey" style. This consisted of a hill; (either natural or artificial) called the "Motte" on which the central tower, or keep, was built. The "Bailey" was the courtyard area formed by the outer walls. The central tower was at the top of the hill, and the castle walls are more or less where we see them today.

During the 1170's Henry II rebuilt the central tower and walls in stone, and also added what are now the Royal Apartments. Although it is known as the "Round Tower", the central tower is definitely not cylindrical. It is not your eyes playing you up, it really is not round. It is more of a lumpy oval that can be clearly seen on any of the plans of the castle grounds.

The next major changes were instigated by Edward III. He had founded the "Knights of the Garter" in 1348 and he added the St.George's Hall for the use of the members of the Order. The Hall is decorated with the coats of arms of past and present members of the Order.

The magnificent St.George's Chapel is one of the finest examples of medieval architecture in the world. It is more of a miniature cathedral than a chapel. Ten former kings lie buried in the chapel: Edward IV,

Henry VI, Henry VIII, Charles I, George III, George IV, William IV, Edward VII, George V and George VI.

Oliver Cromwell captured Windsor Castle early on in the dispute, shortly after the Battle of Edgehill in 1642. This became a Parliamentary stronghold and headquarters for the New Model Army.

After the Restoration of the Monarchy in 1660 Charles II set out to develop the castle into a showpiece. The Palace of Versailles was being constructed at the same time and Charles was determined not to be outdone. The new State Apartments were constructed, and no expense was spared with elaborate murals, ceilings and decorative carvings. The paintings purchased for decoration developed into the present "Royal Collection" that now contains over 7,000 paintings, 40,000 watercolours and drawings, and around 150,000 prints. That is not to mention all of the furniture, ceramics and other works of art.

The next major development came with George IV in the 1820's. The principal architect was Sir Jeffry Wyatville who refashioned the exterior appearance in Gothic style with the addition of turrets and towers.

Victoria and Albert spent much of their time at Windsor. They had a somewhat easier journey to London than their predecessors for now they had the railway to get them there and back again. It was during Victoria's reign that the castle was first opened up to the public.

In 1861 Albert died of typhoid while at Windsor Castle. Victoria had a mausoleum built at Frogmore in the nearby Windsor Home Park.

The last major development at Windsor Castle came about by accident. On 20th November 1992 a fire started in the Private Chapel. It is believed to have been caused by a hot spotlight igniting a curtain. The resulting blaze took fifteen hours to extinguish with over one and a half million gallons of water pumped out of the Thames in order to douse the flames. Over 20% of the castle area was affected, causing damage to over one hundred rooms.

The restoration process took five years and was the largest historic building project undertaken in the 20th century. The final cost was £37 million. Quite amazingly this was some £3 million under the original budget.

Datchet to Runnymede

The Victoria and Albert Bridges were constructed after an extraordinary piece of sheer bloody-mindedness from Buckinghamshire and Berkshire Councils. The first bridge over the river at Datchet had become unsafe, and in 1811 the Government insisted that a new bridge be built by the counties. However, the two counties could agree on absolutely nothing for the construction of the bridge. They could not agree who was going to build it, what it was going to look like, or even what materials should be used in the construction. This resulted in each of the councils doing their own thing. Buckinghamshire built their half of the bridge on their side of the river in wood, and Berkshire built theirs to a totally different design and used cast iron. The two half-bridges were then joined in the middle. Needless to say this mongrel was pretty useless and only stood for 40 years before being replaced by the first Victoria and Albert Bridges. As the councillors would say these days "Lessons have been learned" and the new bridges were of identical construction. Unfortunately both bridges needed to be rebuilt during the last century, Albert in 1928 and Victoria in 1967, and consequently have different looks again.

The towpath downstream from Victoria Bridge is closed "for reasons of security", which is probably a euphemism for "it's too easy to slip into the back of Windsor Castle if you really want to". Just to make sure that nobody accidentally strays from the prescribed route a security guard stands on the bridge waving at me to signal that I should cross the road if I want to stay out of the dungeons.

The Thames Path follows the road through Datchet, and then crosses back over Albert Bridge to return me to the towpath. The main river turns left and swings around a bend, but the towpath follows the lock cut and shortly I am at Old Windsor Lock

Old Windsor was where Edward the Confessor had a royal palace. There is evidence that the area was popular with royalty well before then, going back to the 9th century. Old Windsor was very convenient for hunting in Windsor Forest, and the river provided a convenient means of travel. It was William the Conqueror who moved the palace three miles upstream to Windsor because he thought it provided a superior strategic position while still allowing easy access to the prime hunting forest.

The "Bells of Ouzeley" is an odd name for a pub. It was mentioned by Jerome K Jerome as a "picturesque inn", but has since been converted to a modern "Harvester". The name refers to an alleged incident during the dissolution of the monasteries. A group* of monks had taken the bells from Osney Church in Oxford and were transporting them down the river to prevent them from falling into the hands of Henry VIII's agents. When they reached this part of the Thames the boat they were using capsized, and the bells were allegedly lost in the mud and never recovered.

(* I searched in vain for a collective noun to use for a group of monks. All I could find was a reference to an "abomination" of monks which did not sound suitable to me. I did find references to a superfluity of nuns and a psalter of bishops which could come in handy one day).

Runnymede and Magna Carta

A short walk along the road and I pass between two Lodge Houses situated on either side of the carriageway. These lodges were designed by Sir Edwin Lutyens to mark the entrance to Runnymede Meadows. The famous meadows are the site of one of the most significant autograph signings in history. It was here that King John is alleged to have signed Magna Carta, "The Great Charter" in 1215.

Exactly where or how this was done is still the subject of much speculation. When asked where Magna Carta was signed any cheeky schoolboy will reply "At the bottom" which is possibly more accurate than anybody else can place it.

Most people take the story of the signing of Magna Carta a little bit too much on trust. It is when you start to think about it a little more deeply that all sorts of questions spring to mind.

Why Runnymede in the first place? Why in the middle of a field halfway between Windsor and Staines? There was nothing here then, and there is nothing here now except memorials to Magna Carta. However the name "Runnymede" is thought to come from early Anglo-Saxon roots, "runinge" meaning to take council, and "moed" being a meadow. So was this a historic meeting point well before the reign of King John? There is a school of thought that says that King Alfred used to have regular council meetings here known as the "Witan" when he was resident at Old Windsor, just a short distance upriver.

How did it all come about in the first place? The common misconception is that it went something like this……..

A group of Barons had decided that they have had their fill of King John demanding this, that and the other from them and giving them nothing back in return. So they banded together and demanded that John meet them on neutral ground. When they were all gathered together one of the barons said "Right John, we will agree to pay some of these taxes if you stop locking us up without trial. We don't want to pay to go fishing on the Thames neither. Stick your name here and we can all go home".

You are now thinking, hmmmm, it just might have been a little more complicated than that. Just think of a present-day world summit meeting with their thousands of negotiators and back-room support staff. They have computers and all sorts of whizz-kiddery and it takes months of preparation and days of talks to get anywhere. How did they do it all in 1215 in one afternoon when the height of technology was the quill pen?

It will be no great surprise to learn that the school version of Magna Carta is a massive over-simplification.

Firstly, King John did not sign Magna Carta at Runnymede. He placed his seal at the bottom of a draft form of the document called "Articles of the Barons", and as this was properly witnessed under Common Law it became legally binding. The document was not signed (or sealed) by any of the barons. The full Magna Carta, (translation Great Paper) was not sealed until a month later after the Chancery had redrafted it into the final document.

Let's take a more detailed look at the background.

By the end of the 12th century the Norman system of government had enabled the King of England to become the most powerful man in

Western Europe. Power has a nasty habit of going to ones head and King John was no exception. I have already discovered during the course of my journey that John was not one of our better rulers, and he soon started to get things very, very wrong.

John was not the only choice for King when his older brother Richard died. There was also considerable support for Richard's nephew, Arthur of Brittany. To secure the throne of England John needed the support of the King of France, Philip Augustus. In order to help Philip decide to support his claim to the crown, John gave the King of France a large portion of the lands he held in Anjou. Big mistake.

In every really big mess, there always has to be a woman involved somewhere. The woman in this case was Isabella of Angouleme who John had taken rather a shine to and decided to marry. Isabella's jilted fiancée, Hugh IX of Lusignan, did not take this too well, and appealed to Philip to help him get his revenge on John. Philip immediately declared all the remainder of John's French lands to be forfeit, invaded them with his army and gave them to Arthur of Brittany to rule over.

John had to act to save face, and despatched his armies across to France to grab his lands back. His French barons were not exactly supportive, for Arthur of Brittany had suddenly died in mysterious circumstances. You can guess who (probably correctly) was getting all the blame. John's allies (what was left of them) were defeated at the Battle of Bouvines and the lands were finally conceded to France. The revenue from these lands had previously generated a significant part of the crown income, and put a severe hole in the budget. John decided to squeeze the Barons for more taxes to make up the shortfall, so tightening the pressures that would lead to the revolt.

There was no constitutional crisis in the medieval days that the involvement of the Church could not make considerably worse. It's about time we looked at their contribution to this hiatus. The appointment of the Archbishop of Canterbury had always been a contentious issue, but took a new turn following the crowning of King John.

Until 1200 the Archbishop had been selected by the monarchy in consultation with the monks of Canterbury. Now the monks wanted more say, and elected one of their number to be the new Archbishop. John responded by sending John de Gray, Bishop of Norwich to Rome as his appointed Archbishop. The Pope, Innocent III, decided that he would have neither of them and persuaded the monks to elect Stephen Langton instead. Upon hearing this John completely threw his teddy out of the pram and ordered all of the Canterbury monks into exile. The Pope hit back, and ordered an interdict, whereby all acts of worship, mass, marriages and even the ringing of church bells were declared illegal in England from 1208. When John did not respond, Innocent upped the ante by excommunicating the King in 1209. After receiving no response from this action, the Pope started to encourage Philip of France to invade and conquer England. John eventually backed down, and agreed to have Bishop Langton as Archbishop and allowed the monks to return. To further placate the Pope, he also gave England and Ireland to become Papal Territories and rent them back. The Barons were not happy about this at all, seeing it as selling out to the Papal powers.

So now we have land, power, women and religion all in the melting pot. All we need to do now is add a few money problems and the whole lot will go bang. Which is exactly what happened.

The state income was devastated and tax revenues were required to finance the wars necessary to win back the lost lands. John used all the trickery and double-talk he could to raise the levels of taxation. He re-interpreted Forest Law, which applied to hunting rights in the Royal Forests. He increased by several fold the taxes in scutage, which was the payment of taxes instead of providing military service, and worst of all he introduced a form of income tax, that was as popular then as its descendant is today.

The Barons had suffered enough, and together they marched on London. Such was the unpopularity of John that the city threw its gates open in welcome to them. The combined forces of the Barons were enough for John to meet them at Runnymede and put his seal to "The Articles of the Barons" on June 15th 1215. Magna Carta. On June 19th the Barons responded by re-affirming their fealty to King John.

The Chancery then took the various clauses and made them into Magna Carta. Several copies were made and distributed to the Barons, Royal Sherrifs and Bishops.

The major cause of concern to John was clause number 61. This clause was the longest part of the document, and the part that everyone knows something about. It established a committee of 25 barons who could meet at any time and over-rule the King, even to the extent of confiscating his property.

All the way through the process John had been unable to take any situation without making it a whole lot worse, and as soon as the barons had left London he was at it again. He renounced the clause, and England was plunged into yet another civil war, the First Barons' War.

John died in 1216 and his son Henry III succeeded to the throne. This is where William Marshall, who we discovered at Caversham a few days ago, comes into play. He, as we have learned, was Henry's Regent, and he set about revising Magna Carta to keep the peace. On November 12th

1216 the revised Magna Carta, without clause 61 was issued, followed by further revisions in 1217 and 1225, by which time it had been reduced to 37 clauses.

The version of Magna Carta so often quoted in English Law is the final version, which was issued by Edward I on October 12th 1297, just over eighty years after the original version. Every King for the next two hundred years included the charter of 1297 in their charters until Henry V put an end to the practice.

At the present day only three of the clauses of 1297 remain in their original form, clauses 1, 19 and 28. Clause 1 guarantees the freedom of the Church of England, Clause 9 covers the ancient liberties of the City of London and Clause 29 guarantees a right to due process by the law.

> Clause I. *"First, We have granted to God, and by this our present Charter have confirmed, for Us and our Heirs forever, that the Church of England shall be free, and shall have all her sole Rights and Liberties inviolable. We have granted also, and given to all the Freemen of our Realm, for Us and our Heirs forever, these Liberties under-written, to have and to hold to them and their Heirs, of Us and our Heirs forever."*

> Clause IX. *"The City of London shall have all the old Liberties and Customs which it hath been used to have. Moreover We will and grant, that all other Cities, Boroughs, Towns and the Barons of the Five Ports, and all other Ports, shall have all their Liberties and free Customs."*

> Clause XXIX *"No Freeman shall be taken or imprisoned, or be disseissed of his Freehold, or Liberties, or free Customs, or be outlawed, or exiled, or any other wise destroyed; nor will We not pass upon him, nor condemn him, but by lawful judgment of his Peers, or by the Law of the Land. We will sell to no man; we will not deny or defer to any man either Justice or Right".*

Where on these meadows it all happened is anybody's guess. There is a school of thought that says it was not on the meadows at all, but on Magna Carta Island which is reached from the opposite bank. It would certainly have been a more strategic place for meeting a slippery rascal like King John. Being an island would have made it more difficult for John to spring any nasty tricks and surprises such as his troops suddenly appearing midway through the proceedings before the Barons had a chance to defend themselves. During the time of Magna Carta the island was used by the nunnery of Ankerwyke and it could be that this was the place where John and the Barons met because both sides could feel relatively safe on the confined island.

So that was Magna Carta, and a fine memorial exists in the National Trust grounds to commemorate it. The Runnymede Memorials are a short walk from the car park. It is with some surprise that I discover that the Magna Carta Memorial is not anywhere near as old as I had assumed it would be.

There are three memorials overlooking the Thames at Runnymede. The oldest is towards the top of the hill. It is administered by the Commonwealth War Graves Commission and is dedicated to the memory of the men and women of the Allied Air Forces who died during the Second World War. This fine memorial was designed by Sir Edward Maufe and unveiled by the Queen on 17th October 1953. Over the entrance there is a dedication; "In this cloister are recorded the names of 20,456 airmen who have no known grave. They died for freedom in raid and sortie over the British Isles and the land and seas of northern and western Europe."

The Magna Carta Memorial was built by the American Bar Association from donations from over 9,000 American lawyers. This memorial is in the shape of a domed classical temple containing a pillar which carries the inscription; "To commemorate Magna Carta, symbol of Freedom Under Law". Sir Edward Maufe also designed this memorial. It was unveiled on 18th July 1957, a mere 742 years after the event it commemorates. There are visitor information plaques displaying the coats of arms of the twenty-five Barons and Bishop Langton accompanied by a brief description of Magna Carta for the benefit of visitors.

The third memorial stands on one acre of ground that is now the property of the United States of America. This memorial was designed by G.A.Jellicoe and unveiled by the Queen on 14th May 1965. It is dedicated to the memory of John F Kennedy who was assassinated on 22nd November 1963. The inscription reads "This acre of ground was given to the United States of America by the people of Britain in memory of John F Kennedy, born 19th May 1917: President of the United States 1961-63: died by an assassin's hand 22nd November 1963. "Let every National know, whether it wishes us well or ill, that we shall pay any price, bear any burden, meet any hardship, support any friend or oppose any foe, in order to assure the survival and success of liberty": from the inaugural address of President Kennedy, January 1961."

The rains of the previous days have stopped, and today is a bright and glorious sunny day. It has brought out the picnickers in full force all the way along the meadows and the riverside car parks are full. It is a very popular location.

Staines

A significant marker appears that makes me realise that my surroundings are soon going to become very urban. I am passing under the worlds biggest car park; the M25. This is it then, I am in London as defined by the big blue line on the road map.

There are other markers to tell me I am in the big city. A white iron post by the towpath is a "coal post", warning merchants that beyond this point they are liable to a levy on coal under an act passed in 1831. It must be an early forerunner of Cuddly Ken's much-hated congestion charge. The post seems to shout "Go past this point and we will have some money off you!" The third marker is a replica of the original "Staines Stone" that marked the upstream limit of the authority of the City of London.

The stone at Staines is a significant marker on the River Thames. In the familiar fashion that we have seen elsewhere on this journey, such markers are all about power and ownership, coupled with restricting powers and ownerships from the general hoi-polloi.

Until 1350 the English Crown held the right to fish all of the rivers in England and charged for licenses for people to trap the fish. Some of the rights, however, had already been sold well before this time. Richard I was in desperate need to finance his part of the Third Crusade and in 1197 he sold the rights to fish all of the lower tidal reaches of the Thames to the City of London in perpetuity. The Staines Marker Stone was erected in 1285 to mark the upstream limits of these rights. Every year until the beginning of the 20th century the Lord Mayor would lead a procession upstream to touch the stone with his sword to re-affirm the fishing rights of the City of London.

Chertsey to Shepperton

The pathway again follows the roads alongside the river all the way through Staines until I reach Penton Hook Lock. The "hook" is an impressive full loop in the river, forming a pear-shaped island to the south. The river followed the loop until the very early nineteenth century; with erosion making the neck ever narrower, until finally the waters broke through and boats were able to take the short-cut across the top. The lock was installed in 1815 and the island has been allowed to take on a wild appearance.

From Penton Hook to Chertsey the towpath becomes narrow, forcing its way between the river on one side and the road on the other. With the number of people on the path today progress is somewhat slower than my normal pace as I shuffle around people coming in the opposite direction and try to overtake those who are forming a slow procession moving in the same direction.

Chertsey Meadow is the last water meadow on the Thames. Almost a constant feature of the upper and middle reaches this is the last one I will pass through. On the opposite bank a new view begins, one which will be very common over the following two days. Bungalows and boat-houses line the opposite bank. An idyllic location in the nice weather, but what happens when the river waters rise? There will be miles of these dwellings just a few feet above the water level and I wonder whether they are able to obtain insurance.

I soon reach Shepperton. This part of the Thames was originally a tangle of incoming waters and islands that made navigation very difficult and took a long time to pass through. There is a ferry to take the walker to the opposite bank, but I am going to award myself a little cheat here. I am stopping for the day, and will be starting tomorrow from the opposite

Weybridge bank. The next three days will take me through our capital city and some very different surroundings.

DAY TEN

SHEPPERTON TO RICHMOND

14.3 Miles

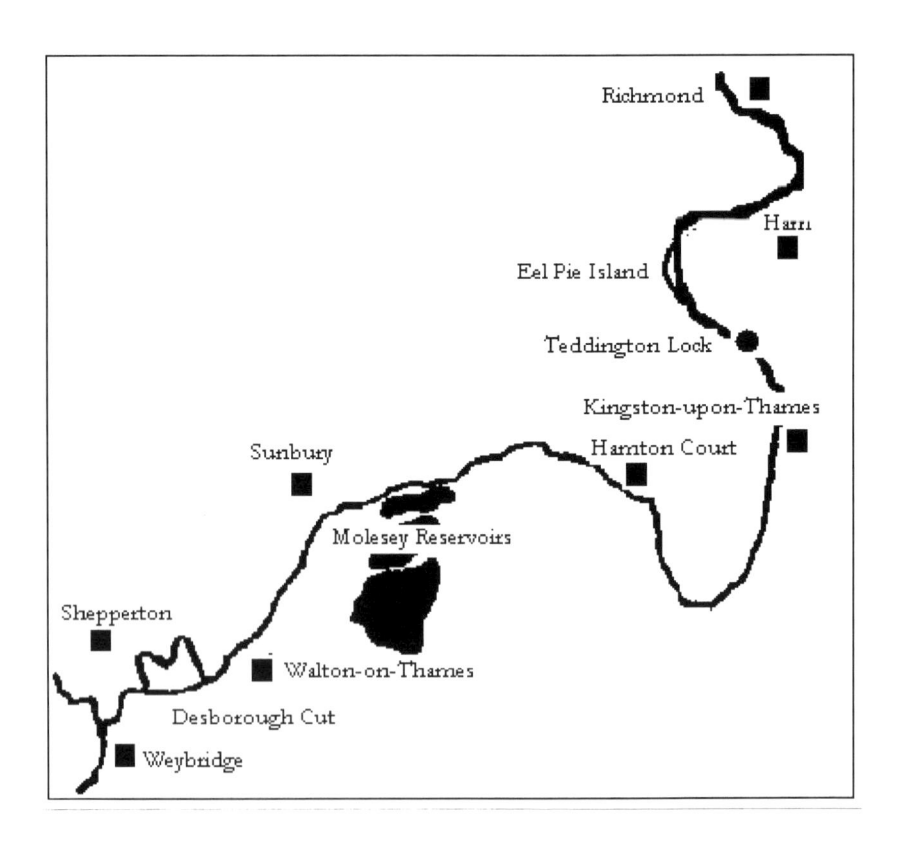

Richard D'Oyly Carte

The first island after Shepperton is known as D'Oyly Carte Island, named after the famous impresario and hotelier of the Victorian era. Its former name was Folly Eyot until Richard D'Oyly Carte purchased the island and built a large house upon it. The house came about a little by accident for his original intention was to use it as an annexe for his very successful Savoy Hotel, but the local magistrates refused to grant a drinks licence and so he used the building as his home instead. The island is now accessed by a bridge, but before 1964 visitors to the island had to ring a bell and be transported by boat.

Carte (May 3rd 1844 to April 3rd 1901) was brought up in the midst of culture. His father was a flautist, music publisher and instrument maker and as a consequence young Richard was an accomplished violinist and flautist from an early age.

During his twenties he wrote and published music for his own songs and instrumentals and four comic operas. While he was having success with his own works he was also building up a successful concert management agency.

In 1875 he became manager of the Royalty Theatre in Soho and this was the start of his great success. The first show he put on was Offenbach's "La Perichole" which was a rather short work. To fill out the programme he asked William Gilbert and Arthur Sullivan to write a comic opera to pad things out a bit. They duly obliged and wrote "Trial by Jury" which became an instant hit with the theatre-going public.

Carte could see the future, and the future he saw was a roaring success for the comic opera. He found some financial backers and formed the Comic Opera Company to produce the further works of Gilbert and

Sullivan. The first opera the company produced was "The Sorcerer" first staged in 1877, followed a year later by "HMS Pinafore".

There was a deepening disagreement between the owners, which at one point descended into an attempt by his former partners to disrupt a performance. Eventually Carte tired of the constant bickering and formed the D'Oyly Carte Opera Company to become the sole producer of Gilbert and Sullivan Operas.

With the money coming in from the success of the operas, coupled with the profits from the concert agency, there was a healthy surplus for investment in other ventures. Carte chose to invest in real estate and purchased property along the Strand. He built the Savoy Theatre in 1881, and in 1889 opened the Savoy Hotel. He chose the name from history, for the Savoy Palace once stood on the same ground until it was burned down during the Peasants Revolt of 1381.

The elegant Savoy Hotel rapidly became famous for its luxury and the upper-classes flocked through its doors. The money generated by the hotel was greater than the rest of the D'Oyly Carte enterprises put together. Carte was like a Monopoly player in full flow. Buy a hotel, get more money, and buy another hotel. He bought and developed Claridges in 1894, Simpsons-in-the-Strand in 1898 and The Berkeley in 1901.

Carte was a tremendous innovator, and would embrace anything that attracted people to his productions and hotels. His Savoy Theatre was the first public building to be illuminated entirely by electric light. (Another piece of trivia for the quiz buffs).

When the licence was refused for his hotel on Folly Eyot, Carte chose to live there himself. What gatherings there must have been on this island towards the end of the 19th century. Richard Carte was the Simon Cowell of late Victorian England. He had all the contacts and ran all of the top shows. The great entrepreneur then doubled up again because where else would the cream of Society go after his shows but to stay in one of his luxury hotels. He certainly had a system.

The Desborough Cut

Between Shepperton and Walton Bridge the natural river forms a sweeping "M" shape. This acted as something of a buffer causing low flow rates further downriver leading to silting of the river. This difficulty was resolved by the digging of the "Desborough Cut", opened in 1935. It is named after Lord Desborough, who was the longest serving chairman of the Thames Conservancy.

The Desborough Cut joins the bases of the "M" with a straight line, forming an island in the middle that is logically named Desborough Island. Digging the cutting not only improved the flow-rates for which purpose it was designed, but more importantly for my current purposes provides a short-cut reducing the distance to Walton-on-Thames by more than half.

Baron Desborough was a very interesting character whose life seems to leap out at you from the pages of a "Boys Own" comic. You know the sort of thing, up early in the morning, do lots of good deeds and only just getting to the stadium in time to win a gold medal after all the other competitors had already started.

William Henry Grenfell was born on October 30th 1855. His father was Charles William Grenfell a former Member of Parliament for Sandwich. The young William excelled at sports, setting a record for the mile at Harrow School that was to stand for sixty years before being beaten.

Sporting excellence continued when he went to Balliol College, Oxford. Grenfell rowed twice in the Boat Race, including the famous "dead heat" race of 1877. He was elected President of the Oxford University Athletics Club in 1876, and President of the Oxford University Boat Club in 1878. Later he turned his attentions to punting, and won the Upper Thames Punting Championships for three successive years, 1888, 1889 and 1890. In 1906 he was part of the British Olympic team that took part in the Interim Games held in Athens, and led the British team to a silver medal in the epee fencing competition.

Not content with victories against fellow beings, he also tested himself against the forces of nature. He swam across the base of Niagara Falls on two occasions, and as if that was not enough he climbed the Matterhorn on three separate occasions and rowed across the English Channel.

William Grenfell dedicated himself to public service in a way that we would not consider today. He stood for Parliament and was elected as a Liberal member for Salisbury in 1880 and 1885, and for Hereford in 1892. In 1893 he resigned his seat because he felt he could not support Gladstone's Irish Home Rule Bill. However he returned to Parliament in 1900 as a Conservative and represented High Wycombe for five years before he was elevated to the Peerage as Baron Desborough in 1905.

All in all this looks quite a full life, but that was not enough for him. It seems that he was a classic example of the old adage "If you want something done ask a busy man, because they are the only people that have the time". So stand by, this is what he did in his spare time; President of the Amateur Fencing Association; President of Marylebone Cricket Club; President of the Lawn Tennis Association; President of the London Chamber of Commerce; President of the Royal Agricultural Society; and

President of the Thames Conservancy for a period of thirty-two years during which he planned and oversaw the cutting that bears his name.

I am only pausing for breath; I will continue……… Mayor of Maidenhead; Steward of the Henley Royal Regatta; Chairman of the British Olympic Association from 1905 to 1913 and to cap it all he was Chairman of the committee that organised the 1908 London Olympic Games.

Desborough's family life was to prove one of sadness. Two of his sons, Julian and Gerald, were killed in action during the First World War, and his youngest son Ivor was killed in a mooring accident in 1926. Upon his death in 1945 the title of Lord Desborough ceased to exist.

Swan Upping

There is a short stretch of the towpath at Sunbury that is marked as a "swan-feeding" area. As you can imagine this is extremely popular, not only with the children who delight in the attention that a swan will give to anybody who throws some food towards it, but also with the swans who collect here to greedily receive the free offerings.

The river at Sunbury can be a very busy place at the start of the third week of July. This is where the annual "Swan Upping" census of the swans along the river often starts its ceremonial procession upstream, finally finishing at the end of the week at Abingdon.

The origins of "swan-upping" date back to the 12th century, and like so many activities where officialdom becomes involved was not so much about keeping accurate records of how many swans there were on the river, but rather a means whereby the rich and powerful got to keep everything of value for themselves and prevent others from enjoying the same benefits.

In the early days all swans were deemed to be the property of the crown, and swans would regularly be taken for royal feasting and banqueting. Later, in the 15th century, ownership of the swans was extended to include two livery companies, the Worshipful Company of Vintners and the Worshipful Company of Dyers. The illegal taking of swans brought severe penalties of seven years transportation and even as recently as 1895 the penalty for illegally killing a swan was seven years hard labour.

In times gone by the Dyers would mark their swans by making a nick in the beak, whilst those of the Vintners' Company would be marked with two nicks in the beak. (Hence the seemingly odd pub name "The Swan with Two Nicks"). In a rather neat piece of gamesmanship the Royal Swans would not be marked at all. Depending on your point of view this either shows a humanitarian side to the process by not damaging the swans unnecessarily, or it is part of a devious scam that enabled the crown to also lay claim to any swans that were previously missed during the "upping" because they would not be marked either.

These days the swans are all ringed above the feet with a unique identity to enable more constructive and scientific monitoring of the swan population along the river. The monitoring is carried out by the Zoology Department of Oxford University.

Swan Upping takes place under the direction of the Queen's Swan Marker. The current holder of this position is David Barber. The marker has his own boat with one skuller with a pair of skulls and two rowers each with one oar, while the Queen's Boat and those of the Dyers and Vintners are traditional 25 foot Thames skiffs with two rowers each with a pair of oars. The boats fly distinctive pennants, white with a large E.R. for the Queen, blue for the Dyers and red for the Vintners. To make it easier for identification all the officials wear traditional scarlet uniforms.

The skiffs set off upstream from Sunbury to seek out and ring the new cygnets and examine swans that they have marked in previous years.

When a family of swans is spotted the cry of "All up" is given and the boats surround the birds and start to nudge them towards the riverbank. The skiffs are pulled together to form a solid corral and the swans are trapped. When the birds arrive at the shallows the boatmen jump into the river and attempt to subdue them by tying their legs together. The swans are then checked for health, identified from their ring markings and weighed. The cygnets are given a new identification ring and they too are measured and weighed. Once the whole family have been checked and weighed they are released back to the water and the boats all set off upstream in search of more swans. During the five days the Uppers will probably tag nearly a hundred cygnets.

That is what happens in theory, but the practise is a little more fun. In reality the nice swan does not want to swim to the bank when rudely shoved in that direction by a boat carrying gaudy flags, and he (or she) does not want any man grabbing hold of their legs and tying them together, and they definitely don't want some great big red coat grabbing hold of their dearly loved little cygnets and putting nasty rings on their little legs just like the one that has been annoying mummy for years. The result is a lot of hissing, splashing, aggressive flapping of wings and general mayhem. It must be seen to be believed, and a fair-sized crowd usually follows the swan-uppers as they go about their task.

When the flotilla passes Windsor Castle the crews observe a quaint tradition and all the boatmen stand to attention and raise their oars in a salute to the Queen.

After the week is completed the Queen's Swan Marker will produce a full report including weights and health of each bird that will be used as a census for improving the conservation of the swan population of the river.

The Swan Marker is not just a job for a week, it goes on all year. The marker is also responsible for continually monitoring the swans on the Thames, and also for removing them from areas before regattas and other events that would cause the swans some stress if they were allowed to remain.

Tagg's Island and Fred Karno

Before I reach Molesey Lock, the largest on the non-tidal river, there is one more delight in store. A series of houseboats stretched along a row of islands in the middle of the river cannot fail to attract ones attention.

The largest of these islands is Tagg's Island, named after Tom Tagg, who was an entrepreneurial boat builder who invested the money from his boat business on the island to a include a hotel which became extremely popular with the arts and entertainments branches of society.

But it is the man who he sold it to who is of most interest. Mr Frederick John Wescott, music hall entertainer without equal in his day. He was better known to our grandparents and great-grandparents as Fred Karno.

Yes indeed; the man who gave us Fred Karno's Army, a name that even today is still a byword for any chaotic group of people. His stock in trade was the slapstick comedy sketch of the music-hall, and he was the absolute master of it. Karno invented the "custard-pie-in-the-face" gag, still used by clowns throughout the world. He soon realised that there was far more money to be made by organising the sketches and managing the performers. The on-stage antics of his performing troupes reduced audiences to tears and the halls were packed whenever one of his touring teams came to visit. Early members of his troupes included the young Charlie Chaplin and Stan Laurel. His later discoveries included Stanley Powell, Flanagan and Allen and the incomparable Max Miller.

The name "Fred Karno's Army" originated from an irreverent World War One marching song. This little ditty was a reference to General Kitchener's hastily trained and usually shambolic "New Army", of which some wag had said "Kitchener's Army; more like Fred Karno's Army", and the name has stuck for nearly a hundred years.

We are Fred Karno's Army, the ragtime infantry.
We cannot fight, we cannot shoot, what bleeding use are we?
And when we get to Berlin we'll hear the Kaiser say,
"Hoch! Hoch! Mein Gott, what a bloody rotten lot, are the ragtime infantry"

We are Fred Karno's Army, the ragtime infantry.
Fred Karno is our Captain, Charlie Chaplin is our O.C.
But when we get to Berlin we'll hear the Kaiser say,
"Hoch! Hoch! Mein Gott, what a bloody rotten lot, are the ragtime infantry".

Hampton Court Palace

Hampton Court Palace is one of only two palaces remaining that were built in the reign of Henry VIII. The other is St James's Palace.

We will start the tale with Thomas Wolsey. Was this man ever ambitious? There may never have been a more ambitious man in the whole history of England. He was a wheeler-dealer without equal who makes modern politicians look a bunch of amateurs in comparison. Inevitably he got his come-uppance at the end, but when he was in full cry............

Thomas Wolsey was born in Ipswich in 1470. His father was Robert Wolsey, a wealthy cloth merchant who was later to die at the Battle of Bosworth Field. The young Wolsey attended Ipswich School, Magdalene College School and Magdalene College where he studied theology. He was ordained into the priesthood in 1498. So there he was, twenty eight years old and a priest, a fairly normal life in those days for sons of the relatively well-off. What he did in today's whizz-kid thinking was to have a career plan that reached for the stars. He decided that he would "really go for it".

Wolsey became a Master at Magdalene School and very quickly became Dean of Divinity. He was starting to get a grip on the greasy pole.

In 1502 he became Chaplain to the Archbishop of Canterbury and it looked as though he was moving up well. Unfortunately for Wolsey the Archbishop died the following year, and he started again by becoming Estate Manager to Sir Richard Nanfan. When he died in 1507 Wolsey had become sufficiently noticed to be taken into the service of Henry VII and the career progression moved up a few gears.

Henry VII was distrustful of the nobility and tended to favour the support of those who had proved themselves to be capable from the more modest families. It was the same logic that the mill owners were later to use when they set up Grammar Schools to educate the sons of their workers, proving that there is nothing new and we can learn from history. (Someone please tell the present Government). Thomas Wolsey fitted this to the proverbial "T" and with his drive and organisation ability he soon established himself with the King.

When Henry VIII came to the throne he gave Wolsey a seat on the Privy Council, and he had "lift-off"!

Henry did not keep such a close eye on his counsellors as did his predecessor and Wolsey took full advantage. He became the most powerful man in England and was accumulating great wealth (as they do). In 1514 he purchased the lease on the manor house at Hampton and set about transforming it into the greatest palace in the land.

His ecclesiastical career was also in full flow. He had already reached the high office of Bishop of Lincoln, then to Archbishop of York, and in 1515 Pope Leo X appointed him a Cardinal which meant that in the eyes of the church he held a higher status than the Archbishop of Canterbury. In the early fifteenth century England you really could not get much higher. Direct communication with both the King and the Pope gave almost unlimited powers. So long as his two masters could be kept satisfied Wolsey was the top man. So long as his masters were happy and did not fall out Wolsey had it made. But of course they did fall out. Big time.

Wolsey wheeled and dealed. He even brokered Henry's sister Mary in marriage to Louis XII to secure a treaty with France. When Louis died Wolsey then pursued an alliance with Spain and the Holy Roman Empire to fight against the French. When this went wrong Wolsey then set about renegotiating another treaty with France which resulted in probably his greatest diplomatic triumph, "The Field of the Cloth of Gold" in 1520. On the face of it this gave England a new arrangement with France, but Wolsey was more duplicitous than that and used the opportunity to play the French off against the Spanish. As soon as everyone had gone home thinking that all was well between England and France, our friend Wolsey had done a deal with Charles V of Spain.

France did not accept this with a Gallic shrug, light up a Galloise and say "C'est la vie". They set about an alliance with the Scots to cause as much trouble as they could on England's northern borders.

All went well for a few years until France and Spain agreed a peace treaty that left England once more on the sidelines.

I do hope you are keeping up with the plot because it is going to start getting a lot messier. We have the battles for power, we have the money, we have the Church, and so what is the only thing needed to complete the tinder box? Correct; a woman.

Henry had married Catherine of Aragon to reinforce the treaty with Spain, Catherine being the aunt of Charles V. The marriage had only produced a daughter, Mary, who was destined to cause a fair amount of mayhem herself in her adult years. The one thing about Mary that Henry was sure of was that she would not be accepted as the unopposed ruler on his death, and that all the old rivalries that had caused the "Wars of the Roses" would resurface once more.

To Henry there was a simple answer. Get the marriage to Catherine annulled and marry the lovely Ann Boleyn who would straight away produce a son and heir. Job done. Wolsey could probably fix it before lunchtime.

Wolsey had a big problem. Even the most expert "spin doctor" was going to have an impossible job justifying the sort of "trumped up" nonsense that Henry was coming up with as valid reasons for the annulment. Charles V was not going to agree in any way with the annulment of his aunt's marriage. Pope Clement VII was on a loser whatever he did. He could either upset Henry or Charles and he could not afford to do either. So he did what all politicians have done throughout the ages when faced with a similar predicament, he did nothing.

Henry went ballistic and blamed Wolsey for everything. Wolsey's world came crashing down around him. Henry stripped Wolsey of his Government Offices and all of his properties, including the palace, which Henry took for his own residence. He allowed Wolsey to keep the office of Archbishop of York and the Cardinal headed north in disgrace. When he arrived there he was accused of treason and arrested by the Earl of Northumberland to be taken to London. Wolsey was distraught. He had done everything for his King but one final, impossible demand. On the journey to London he fell severely ill and died at Leicester on November 29th 1530.

Henry was delighted with his new "acquisition" and moved his residence from the Palace of Westminster to Hampton Court. He continued to extend the building, adding the Great Hall and also the celebrated "Real Tennis" Court.

Between 1689 and 1694 during the reign of William and Mary the palace was subjected to a huge renovation project and half of the original works were replaced. The architect was Sir Christopher Wren who was responsible for the south façade and the addition of two wings to the palace. Further renovations were carried out by George I and George II.

George III did not share his predecessors' love of Hampton Court, and from then on the palace ceased to be a royal residence, the monarchy preferring other London homes.

The palace is allegedly haunted by the ghost of Catherine Howard, the fifth wife of Henry VIII, who is reputed to walk the area known very appropriately as "The Haunted Gallery". In 1541 Catherine was accused of adultery and placed under house arrest at Hampton Court. The story is that she escaped from her guards and ran down the gallery looking for the King so that she could plead for her life. She was caught by her guards who dragged the screaming Catherine back along the gallery to her rooms.

Over the years unidentified screams have been reported from the gallery, and several visitors have claimed to have been affected in some way whilst in the gallery. In 1999 two female visitors fainted in exactly the same spot on the floor of the gallery just half an hour apart.

Inevitably Jerome visited Hampton Court Palace on his journey up the Thames, and tells us the story of Harris and the maze.

The maze was planted sometime between 1689 and 1695 by George London and Henry Wise as part of a wilderness garden for William of Orange. The maze was originally constructed of hornbeam, but has been replanted several times over the years. The current maze is built with yew hedges. There are over half a mile of paths in the maze.

Jerome's character Harris assured everyone that it was but just a few minutes to solve the maze, all you had to do was to keep turning right. Harris was almost correct, for the maze can theoretically be negotiated by the relatively simple means of always ensuring that you keep the hedge on your right, and turning accordingly. This will get you into the centre and out again with only a few short diversions. So much for the theory, I just had to try it out in practice, and I am delighted to say that it works a treat.

Shortly after passing the palace buildings I come to the rather splendid 18th century screen by Tijou that allows me to see into the privy garden and across to the south wing. The screen unfortunately is somewhat obscured by protective railings, no doubt essential to afford protection against the aerosol paint sprayers of the area.

Kingston-upon-Thames

From Hampton Court Bridge the river makes a giant loop to the south, sweeping back up again around the grounds of the Palace. The footpath becomes rather more grandiose than a simple towpath, and becomes a wide stoned pathway known as the Barge Walk. A very pleasant walk it is to, and I merrily stroll along with the parkland to my left and the river flowing alongside on my right. Soon Kingston Bridge comes in sight. The grassy areas to the sides of the path are populated with people spending their lunch-hour sitting out in the spring sunshine.

The day visitor to the area can make this last section from Hampton Court into a circular walk by following the A308 from Kingston Bridge back across the top of the loop to Hampton Court.

Kingston Bridge marks an end point of sorts, for I can now get rid of some baggage that has been with me since the dreaming spires of Oxford. At some point over the last couple of minutes I have passed the point where Jerome K Jerome set off with Harris and George (not to mention Montmorency the dog) on their adventure. "Our boat was waiting for us at Kingston, just below the bridge". So he has gone, and another section of my journey ends. I am now in a "Jerome -free zone".

Believe it or not I am only ten miles from central London according to the proverbial flying crow. However, the sweeping bends of the waterway through the capital require me to cover almost twice that distance before I reach Westminster Bridge.

Kingston was formed at the first crossing point of the Thames upstream of London Bridge. The town goes back to Roman times, and later there is a record of a great council being held her in 838 under the ruling of Egbert of Wessex.

The town really came into its own when it was chosen as the location for the coronation of seven Saxon Kings, starting with Edward the Elder in 900AD. The next four Saxon Kings were also crowned at Kingston, Athelstan (924), Edmund I (939), Edred (946) and Edwy (955). Two other Kings received their crowns at Kingston, Edward the Martyr (975) and Ethelred the Unready (991). They were all believed to be crowned using the Coronation Stone that now sits proudly outside the guildhall, with the names of the Kings carved around the base.

The origin of the town name is somewhat in dispute, so make up your own minds. One argument says that it is simply a derivative of King Stone from the coronations, and another says that it is from an earlier Saxon root being Kings Tun, meaning farmstead of the Kings. Both seemed very logical until I found another reference that it was called Kyningestun at the time of Egbert of Wessex in 838, which would dispel the coronation theory. If you are not confused already, then the good old Domesday Book will assist. In 1086 it recorded the town as Chingestone. However by 1200 King John granted a town charter and it was back to Kingston again.

Enough of the serious business lets get down to some quiz trivia. What was the name of the dog that used to sit by the wind-up gramophone on the famous "His Master's Voice" advertisements? More to the point, what has it to do with Kingston? The answer is that "Nipper" the dog was buried in 1905 underneath what is now Lloyd's Bank, and a commemorative plaque marks the spot for posterity.

Almost immediately after the bridge is Turk's Pier. Surprisingly enough it has nothing to do with a native of that country, but denotes what must be one of the oldest business families in England still running what was basically the original business.

To say that the Turk family have been in the boat building and river transport business for a few generations is something of an understatement. They go way back to the days of the Crusades, building every sort of boat imaginable for use on the waterway including fishing boats, skiffs, pleasure craft and passenger ferries. There is a record in 1185 of a Turk building two galleys near to the Tower of London. Another Turk, also a shipwright was Lord Mayor of London in 1230. The present business was established in 1710 by Richard Turk, whose great-great-great grandson, also named Richard Turk, runs the business today.

On to Canbury Gardens, an attractive tree-lined riverside park maintained by the local council. It is hard to imagine that it is all artificial, being reclaimed from marshland by the dumping of building waste in the late 19th century. It is a very pleasant haven away from the bustling suburbs, and today is full of mums and tots and countless others enjoying a nice spring afternoon. The park was used as a filming location for Dr Who in 1973, but on this occasion no police box appeared to shatter the peace. At the end of the gardens stands "The Boaters Inn" with its wooden tables overlooking the river providing an ideal opportunity for a ham roll washed down with a couple of pints.

Teddington Lock

I am approaching a very significant marker on the walk. This is the end of the non-tidal river. In medieval times the tidal reaches were reckoned to extend as far upstream as Staines, but with the addition of locks the tidal effect now stops at Teddington Lock.

To be precise Teddington should be referred to in the plural, for there are three locks at this location, the Launch Lock, the Barge Lock and the Skiff lock. The three locks make up by far the biggest lock system along the whole of the river.

As I walk towards the locks I can see them laid out before me. The massive Barge Lock 650 feet long was designed to take a steam tug plus six barges and was completed in 1905. The smaller Launch Lock is 178 feet long and was built in 1858. Both of these locks completely dwarf the Skiff Lock, which at a mere 50 feet in length is also known as the "Coffin Lock", presumably an allusion to the claustrophobic feeling that one must have if you are at the bottom of it.

I have to make a decision here because there is a choice for the next two days. The Thames Path splits into two, one following the North Bank and the other the South Bank. I have chosen the South Bank mainly because it appeared to offer more variety, and also because it finished at the Barrier Visitor Centre.

Only a couple of hundred yards below the locks I pass an obelisk. This stone was erected in 1909 and marks the old boundary between the jurisdictions of the Thames Conservancy and the Port of London Authority. It is a significant marker on my journey that brings the thought that I am now on the final count-down to journey's end.

Eel Pie Island

The river is noticeably different below Teddington Lock. The tide is at a half-way point and has exposed gravel beaches along the edges of the water. Gravel or mud beaches will be the common sight for the next two days.

The land to my right is known as the "Ham Lands". During the early part of the twentieth century this area was intensely mined for gravel extraction. A lagoon was formed for loading the gravel on to barges, and this lagoon remains as the sailing area for Thames Young Mariners. The gravel pits were filled with the rubble and waste from the clearance of the London bomb sites; with the result that nature has taken over again and produced an area of wild grassland and plants.

The river sweeps round to the right and another little anachronism appears in view. In the middle of the river sits an island community of tightly-knit houses, studios and workshops marooned in a little sub-world of its own. I have reached the quaintly named "Eel Pie Island".

In earlier days the island was referred to as "Twickenham Ait", the more modern name coming into usage after the celebrated eel pies that were served up at a hotel on the island during the 1800s. There are some tales that the eel pies were famous in Henry VIII's day, but that as may well be, but my money is on this being a superb piece of marketing by some unknown individual intent on gaining publicity for the island's hotel, which they then renamed the "Eel Pie Island Hotel".

The hotel was originally a pub known as "The White Cross" during the 18th century, and was run by Henry Horne, who also doubled-up as the ferryman. The pub was replaced in 1830 by a much larger building, and it was then that the fun started.

However they did it, they did it well. The island soon became what the men from today's pub company marketing teams would call a "Destination Venue". People flocked to spend weekends and evenings on the island, eating and drinking under the trees. It was at this time that the eel pie became famous and used to promote the island. So successful were the pies that the island became known as "Eel Pie Island" and the "White Cross" became the "Eel Pie Island Hotel".

The hotel had a steady time during the early parts of the twentieth century, surviving on ballroom dancing and similar leisurely pursuits, and then the island was connected to the mainland for the first time. They built a bridge in 1957 and the island began to rock.

Eric Clapton, Long John Baldry, The Who, Rolling Stones, Yardbirds, Pink Floyd and many more appeared at the "Eel Pie Hotel" and the place was really jumping. Somehow Mick Jagger calling out "Helloooo Eel Pie" does not have the same ring to it as "Helloooo Rio" but that was way back then. (Bonus point for the pop quiz fans; what was the name of Long John Baldry's only number one hit single?)

The crowds flocked to the venue and many of the artistes became sentimentally attached to the place. Pete Townsend founded Eel Pie Studios and many bands held recording sessions there.

All good things come to an end and the hotel had to close in 1967 because the owner could not afford the necessary repair bills. There was a brief reprise in 1969 when Led Zeppelin and Black Sabbath were among the bands performing at the venue, but then it closed again. In 1971 the hotel mysteriously burned down (as they do) and the island returned to peace and quiet once more.

The island today is home to Twickenham Rowing Club, Richmond Yacht Club and about fifty houses. Its most famous resident is the inventor Trevor Baylis, who invented the wind-up radio.

I continue onwards, sounds of the sixties playing in my brain, in particular the song "Let the Heartaches Begin" which reached No.1 in 1967 for Long John Baldry.

Ham House

Shortly after Eel Pie Island the right hand bank opens up to give an excellent view of Ham House. This is one of the best preserved Stuart houses in Britain, and like many other houses I have passed by along the Thames Pathway it has its own history of people, ambitions and political intrigue. Ham House probably has more than most, and played a key role in the many plots that led to the restoration of the monarchy in the form of King Charles II.

Ham House was built in 1610 for Sir Thomas Vasavour who was Knight Marshall to James I. After Vasavour's death in 1620 the house was purchased by the Earl of Holdernesse, before becoming the home of William Murray in 1626. The young William had an interesting start in life. He was the "whipping boy" for the future Charles I and took all the punishments and beatings incurred by the young prince during his boyhood. Despite, (or maybe because of), all of this one-sided discipline, the two boys formed a strong bond and shared many interests.

During the 1630's Murray extensively developed the interior of the house, adding the Great Staircase and Hall Gallery. The coming of the Civil War saw Murray side with his boyhood chum, and he became a staunch Royalist. As a reward for a lifetime of loyalty he was created 1st Earl of Dysart. He passed away in 1655 and then the real fun began.

The estate and the titles passed to the eldest daughter, Elizabeth. She was described as ambitious, scheming and greedy, and these were the nicer things said about her. Elizabeth was a master of political shenanigans and intrigue. In 1648 she had married Sir Lionel Tollemache, and by the time he died in 1669 she had produced eleven children. Lady Dysart spent much of her time plotting and wheeler-dealing on behalf of the exiled King, and is reputed to have been a leading activist for "The Sealed Knot". Ham House was allegedly used as a centre for all of this activity to restore the monarchy.

Even before the death of her husband, Elizabeth was making advances to the very ambitious John Maitland, 1st Duke of Lauderdale and Secretary of State for Scotland. They married in 1672 and set about making Ham House into the palatial home that the scheming Elizabeth felt she deserved. No extravagance was spared and much of the lavish decoration can still be seen today.

The Duke died in 1682, and Lady Lauderdale continued to rule the house until her own death in 1698. It is said that Lady Lauderdale is still there, continuing her plotting and scheming as she haunts the old house.

Ham House then passed to her oldest son by her first marriage, Lionel Tollemache, 3rd Earl of Dysart. The house passed through several generations of the Tollemache family, until in 1948 Sir Lyonel Tollemache gave the house to The National Trust, who has owned it to the present day.

The gardens are well worth a visit, particularly the Cherry Garden, with its statue of Bacchus as a centre feature. The trees are also a home to a large flock of green parakeets. I thought this was a wind-up when I first heard about it, but this area of West London is full of green parakeets. There are literally thousands of them sitting in the trees. Where they originally came from is the subject of much urban myth. One popular theory is that a container was stolen from Heathrow and when the thieves realized what they had got hold of they just let them go. Another is that they escaped from a bird fancier and naturally bred over many years. Whatever the reason the local environment absolutely suits them to a "T" and since the 1990s the population has boomed.

Alien Invaders

The parakeets are attractive and as far as I am aware do not damage the environment that has contributed to their present numbers. Oh that the same could be said of other species that have made their home here and prospered. I am in the presence of unwanted invaders.

They have been here since 1935, but in the last twenty years they have "bred and spread" up the tidal Thames and are believed to be as far up the river as Staines. The Environment Agency believes that there are tens of thousands of the unwanted invaders causing severe environmental damage to the riverbanks.

The name of this invader of our shores is *Eriocheir sinensis* more commonly known as the Chinese Mitten Crab. It is a medium-sized crab native to South-East Asia. It takes its common name from the dense hairs on its claws that give the impression it is wearing mittens. The body is about the size of the human hand, typically 30 to 100mm across, with its legs approximately twice the length that the body is wide.

The crab probably came to our shores in the holds of ships, and they are now present in the Humber system and the Tyne, and are also becoming an increasing problem on the Rhine and in North West America. If you see a crab in freshwater anywhere in Britain it is almost certainly a mitten crab.

The mitten crab spends most of its life-cycle in freshwater, returning to the sea to breed. When they reach four or five years of age they begin their migration to the sea in late summer and then do whatever it is that mitten crabs do in the estuary waters. After mating the female continues to deeper waters for the winter and returns to the protection of the estuary to lay her eggs. The eggs hatch as larvae, and change into the young crabs which then move upstream in search of freshwater in which to grow.

The environmental damage caused by the severe erosion of the banks as the crabs burrow into them. Not only that, but the damage done to the freshwater fish stocks can be considerable because the crabs eat the fish eggs laid on the river bottom.

In China the crab is considered a great delicacy, but over here they are simply a menace. In common with many shellfish the mitten crab has a great tolerance to polluted environments and wild crabs can be very hazardous to eat.

Richmond

The meadows end and I am back into the built-up area of Richmond. When I say Richmond that is because that is what it says on the map. However it turns out that I have been in Richmond for a very large part of the day already, and still have plenty more to go, for Richmond is deceptive. The place itself looks a fairly standard size for a London suburb on the map, but as is so often the case appearances can be deceptive. The Borough of Richmond is large, and has a population of over 180,000. There are over 100 parks including Richmond Park, Kew, Hampton Court and Ham, plus over twenty-one miles of River Thames frontage. There are over five times as much open space in Richmond than in any other borough in London. It is also the only London borough to have land on both sides of the River Thames. In short it is big.

Richmond is also relatively new. It is believed to have derived its name from the other Richmond in Yorkshire after Henry VII built a palace here in 1500 and called it Richmond Palace. Previously the area was known as Shene, or Sheen.

Henry I was the first royal to live here, spending long periods at the "King's House" in Shene. Edward I developed the house into a royal palace in 1299. The first King to make the palace at Shene his official royal residence was Richard II.

The palace was destroyed by fire in 1497. Henry VII rebuilt it and renamed it Richmond Palace. The glory of Richmond Palace was short-lived, with Henry VIII moving his court upstream to Hampton Court as we discovered earlier.

The path soon changes to a busy neo-classical walkway leading to Richmond Bridge, with a wide promenade. The bridge itself has been in view for a while, with the sun glistening off its five classical Portland stone archways. It was built in 1777 by James Pain and Kenton Couse and was originally a toll bridge. The crossing charge was a halfpenny, but anyone who wanted to push a handcart over the crossing would be charged a full penny.

DAY ELEVEN

RICHMOND TO WESTMINSTER

16.2 Miles

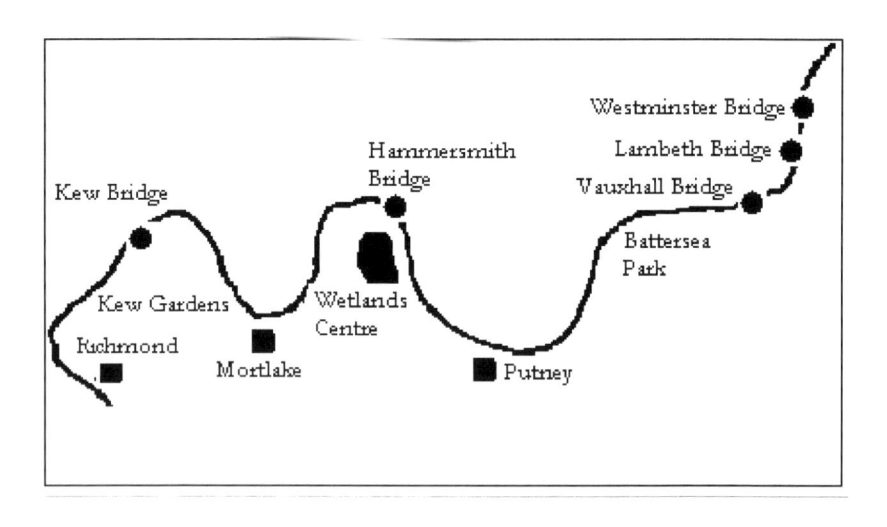

Richmond to Kew

Two days to go, and even the finger-boards alongside the river are showing the countdown to the finish. "Tower Bridge 19" proclaims the sign as I pass under Richmond Bridge.

A short walk takes me under Richmond Railway Bridge and then Twickenham Bridge almost immediately afterwards. Then it is out into open country again, at least on my chosen bank. The opposite bank is Isleworth, but that soon becomes obscured by the island known as "Isleworth Ait", whose covering of trees provides the useful service of blocking out the concrete and brickwork on the land behind.

The open countryside to my right is Old Deer Park, which is mainly put down to playing fields and the fairways and greens of the Royal Mid-Surrey Golf Club. There is an obelisk alongside the pathway with no indication of what it is for. I later discovered that it is a marker point along the meridian line from Kew Observatory which is just visible through the trees. The observatory was built for George III to indulge his hobby of astronomy, and it was completed just in time for him to observe the transit of Venus in 1779. The obelisk I have seen is one of three in Old Deer Park situated north, east and west of the observatory and were used for correctly aligning the telescope. The observatory is used now as a weather station under the control of the Meteorological Office.

The pathway continues with its tree shaded causeway between river and parkland almost all of the way to Kew Bridge.

On the opposite bank there are signs of better days gone by. I am opposite the junction with the Grand Union Canal at Brentford. Once this area was a bustling dockland area, where river barges would exchange cargoes with canal barges that in their turn would make their way up to

Birmingham. Now the area just looks neglected, three boats moored against the entranceway to the lock gate being all that remains.

The area on my right is the famous Royal Botanical Gardens, more commonly referred to simply as Kew Gardens.

Kew hosts the world's largest collection of living plants. There are over 30,000 different species kept here and the site extends to 300 acres.

The gardens are not only for the entertainment of the two million visitors that come here every year, they are also an important botanical research centre with approximately 700 scientists. Kew is considered so important for botanical heritage that it was declared a World Heritage Site in 2003.

Kew had its origins in the garden at Kew Park that was formed by Lord Capel during the later part of the sixteenth century. Capel was an enthusiastic gardener and was renowned for his fruit trees and exotic plants.

Frederick, Prince of Wales, leased the house from 1731. Together with his wife, Augusta and their friend the Earl of Bute they set about enlarging and landscaping the gardens. Frederick died from pleurisy in 1751 and Augusta was determined to complete his plans for the gardens. In 1757 she employed Thomas Chambers to take charge of the developments. The first records of the "Physic and Exotic Garden" date from 1759 and this is accepted as the foundation of the Botanical Gardens.

In 1760 George III came to the throne and continued with the development of the gardens. He employed Capability Brown to transform the landscape and plant many more trees.

The greatest advance for the gardens came in 1797 with the appointment of Sir Joseph Banks to take control. Banks was a celebrated natural historian and botanist who had accompanied Captain Cook on his voyage to Australia. Banks sent out many botanists to search throughout the British Empire to bring back specimen plants for Kew.

The great glasshouses were the design of architect Decimus Burton. The Palm House was opened in 1848, and the Temperate House which is twice the size of the Palm House followed a few years later.

The most recent addition to the gardens is the Xstrata Treetop Walkway. This 200 metre walkway is sixty feet above the ground and provides the visitors with the exhilarating experience of viewing the trees from treetop height.

There is no time to linger in the gardens today, so I pass under Kew Bridge to continue on my way.

Public Records Office

Almost immediately after Kew Railway Bridge there is a very large building on my right that is attempting to hide behind the trees. This building fulfils a very important function for all of us. It is the nation's filing cabinet.

The National Archive holds all of our records for over 900 years from the days of the Domesday Book. It was formed by the merger of the Public Record Office, Historical Manuscripts Commission, Office of Public Sector Information and Her Majesties Stationery Office.

This is much more than simple records of "hatches, matches and despatches". The records cover all public sector, the military, legal aspects, court cases, government, wills, and census. Just about anything that has ever been recorded on parchment, paper, digital or web in England and Wales is here somewhere.

So how big a filing cabinet do we need for all of that lot? Well, it stands on a thirteen acre site and the original building has 33,400 square metres of floor space. It was designed by John Cecil Clavering and completed in 1977. This, however, was nowhere near large enough and an extension was opened in 1995 that added a further 31,750 square metres. Out of all of this a staggering 28,741 is given over to the repository or in simple terms the "filing cabinet".

The records not only need space, but they need carefully looking after. First off, how do they know where everything is? For those of us who have to turn the house upside down every time we have to find some piece of paper that we wrote something down on how would we cope with having nearly 65,000 square metres in which to find it? Haystacks and needles spring to mind. They must have a really good memory to retrieve anything.

When they find what someone is looking for, how do they ensure that it is still in a condition to be of any use? The answer is that the storage areas are incubated, with humidity controlled at 50 degrees and the air temperature at a constant 16 degrees centigrade.

A great many of the records are not actually needed in "hard copy" because they are digitally recorded for easy retrieval and some of the information is readily available online, so you do not have to even visit in person.

Mortlake to Putney

A few yards below Chiswick bridge is the imaginary line across the river where the boat race finishes. For the next four and a quarter miles the walk will follow the course of the famous race, only backwards.

At Henley we saw how the race started with a challenge thrown down by Cambridge. The second race was held at Westminster and in 1845 the race was moved to its present venue between Putney and Mortlake.

The course is very neatly planned and is theoretically perfectly fair. The bird's eye-view of the course is of three great bends in the river, but when you look more closely there is much more to it than that. Both the start and the finish lines are exactly parallel to each other. This means that although each of the bends will give a shorter distance of travel to the boat on the inside of the bend, by the end of the race both boats will have covered exactly the same distance irrespective of whichever side of the river (or station) they have used.

It is the constantly changing nature of the tideway that makes the race a lot more tactical than would first appear. The race is held one hour before high water at Putney. This means that the stream is flowing against the rowers, but the incoming tide is working in their favour. The fastest course to steer depends on a combination of the strength of the tides and the amount of water flowing down the river, which naturally varies with the previous amounts of rainfall through the Thames catchment area. On top of all this comes the wind, which will affect different parts of the course depending on the direction it has chosen to blow on race day. Not only can the wind make conditions very uncomfortable during the race, it can also lead to embarrassment, being one of the major factors in providing the conditions for increasing the chances of one of the boats sinking.

As a measure of how much training techniques and technology have improved over the years, the first race in 1845 was timed at 23 minutes and 30 seconds. The record time set by Cambridge in 1998 is 16 minutes and 19 seconds.

Some of the university rowers that I saw a few days ago upstream at Oxford will have their minds firmly fixed on obtaining a place in the dark-blue boat for next years race. Let's take a look at the hill they have to climb for their (just over) fifteen minutes of fame.

To start with they must already be good oarsmen. Not just good, but very, very, very good. Both universities recruit internationally known athletes to study at their respective institutions. Over the last few years the composition of the crews has increasingly reflected this global outlook.

Secondly they have to be able to put the necessary training work in and keep up their academic courses at the same time. It is estimated that at least two hours of training is taken for each single stroke made during the race. That is some serious commitment.

There is an early test in December when two boats from the same university will race each other along the tideway course. This is known as the "Trial Eights" and gives the coaches an opportunity to evaluate each individual's performances under race conditions.

As the winter progresses the coaches will gradually decide their best teams, and by the end of February will announce the two crews who will contest the main race. Those who just fail to make the grade will be rewarded with a place in the reserve race that takes place half an hour before the big event. The two boats in this race are known as "Isis" (Oxford) and "Goldie" (Cambridge).

Standing here at the finish line I know it is going to take me nearly one hour and a half to get to Putney Bridge. In the boat race they will cover this in around seventeen minutes.

Mortlake brewery may be a noted landmark along the boat race course, but there is little else to merit this next section of towpath. It is narrow, muddy, poorly maintained, and somewhat claustrophobic, with a high brick wall almost literally rubbing my shoulder as I walk. The wall is part of the old brewery and is the subject of a preservation order, though goodness knows why. Ugliness is not a virtue.

A hundred years ago over 1400 workers made this brewery the largest employer in the area and the riverbank would be teeming with barges loading the barrels for distribution around the capital.

Modernisation and changes in distribution methods have reduced this greatly, and the river is no longer used for distribution. The brewery is now much smaller and owned by Stag Breweries.

The bridges are now coming thick and fast as I draw nearer to the centre of London. Hammersmith Bridge is a suspension bridge which I always think gives a sense of grandeur over the standard span bridges.

The first bridge over the river here was designed by our old friend William Tierney Clark who, if you recall, later designed Marlow Bridge. Clark built the very first suspension bridge over the river here in 1827. Traffic over the bridge was very heavy, and it was not many years before there were serious concerns about the strength of the bridge. Things came to a head with the 1870 boat race. The bridge is a splendid vantage point and is situated about halfway along the course. An estimated 12,000 people crowded on to the bridge that year to watch the race, and the local "health and safety" had a fit. Eventually, in 1884, a new bridge was designed by Sir Joseph Bazalgette (1818 – 1891) using the original supporting pillars. The bridge was opened in 1887.

Traffic continued to increase and Hammersmith suffered from more problems over the years. The bridge was completely refurbished in 1973, but additional replacement work was required in 1984 and 1987 to cope with the battering that the shear volume of traffic was giving the structure. In 1997 it was closed for over a year for more structural work and only opened again after the imposition of a weight restriction. The bridge was the target of a terrorist attack in 2000. After this the bridge was completely repainted in the style of the 1887 bridge and looks very well for it as I pass by.

Another boat race landmark appears, the Harrods Depository. The famous store in Knightsbridge no longer uses the premises, but the landmark façade is still preserved. The depository site is now a modern housing development.

London Wetland Centre

A little further along there is something rather more surprising, for here, in the west of London, I find one of the best areas for observing wildlife in the whole of the United Kingdom. This is the "London Wetland Centre".

It is an amazing project. Put simply, the "Wildlife and Wetlands Trust" have taken the old Barn Elms Reservoirs and transformed them into a wildlife haven. In practice it must have involved a tremendous amount of hard work and landscaping. The Trust was founded in 1946 by Sir Peter Scott and currently owns nine wetland centres around the UK. When you consider that over half of the world's natural wetland areas have disappeared during the last hundred years it seems even more amazing that this area of London has been turned back into a wetland and the wildlife has chosen to come to it.

The total area of the London site is 43 hectares, and has nearly two miles of footpaths to enable the visitor to easily access the different parts. There are several "hides" to avoid visitors accidentally frightening away the inhabitants, and smaller ponds enable the visitor to get extremely close to some of the birds.

This reserve turns all of the previous theories about wildlife on its head. Instead of preserving the natural habitat and encouraging visitors to travel to the site this project created an entirely new artificial habitat for the wildlife close to where the people lived, and then waited for the birds to find it.

The Barnes Elms Reservoirs became redundant when the Thames Water ring main came into service. The Wildfowl and Wetlands Trust (WWT) approached Thames Water with a view to converting the reservoirs into a wetland and with the assistance of developer Berkeley Homes they came to an agreement and work began in 1995.

The reservoirs were drained, leaving some water still for the current wildlife. Then the concrete retaining walls were demolished. The concrete was crushed and recycled as foundation materials and pathways. Smaller pools were sculpted into the landscape, all connected by a series of sluice gates that enable delicate control of the water levels.

After two years of landscaping and engineering it was time to start the planting. More than 300,000 aquatic plants, over 2,500 trees and hundreds of water-meadow flowers were planted. Our old friend from North Meadow, the Snakeshead Fritillary, has been successfully planted here and gives a fine display in late spring. Appropriately enough this area of the reserve has been named "Cricklade Fritillary Meadow".

The theory of the city wetland centre was instantly proved to be correct. Wildlife literally flocked to the site, and rapidly established the habitat. There are now over 180 different species of bird, nine species of bats, more than 500 species of butterflies and moths and countless other insects that can be seen at various times of the year. Add a few reptiles and small mammals to this and you can see what a wonderful haven this has become in a very short time.

Craven Cottage

On the opposite bank sits Craven Cottage, the home of Fulham Football Club. The stadium has a capacity of 26,000 and Fulham first moved here in 1896. It seems a strange name for a football ground.

The original Craven Cottage was built for William Craven, the sixth Baron Craven in 1780. It was believed to have stood approximately where the centre of the pitch is now. The area at the time was heavily wooded and had previously been part of a hunting estate. There are many different claims of famous people who lived at the cottage, in fact so many that they all could not possibly have lived there. The cottage had one of those mysterious fires in 1888, and the land lay unused for another six years before Fulham Football Club started to develop it into a football ground.

Craven Cottage witnessed the fastest hat-trick ever scored in league football. On December 26th 1963 Graham Leggat scored three goals within three minutes as Fulham romped home 10-1 against Ipswich Town. As any regular Fulham fans will tell you, not a lot has happened since.

The approach to Putney Bridge is lined with boathouses owned by various rowing clubs. There are bits of boats everywhere. Ropes, oars, wetsuits, trailers and all sorts of boating paraphernalia are all over the place. Road, pathway, slipway and jetty all morph into one and I pick my way through the obstacle course. Almost all of the way from Shepperton the pathway has benefited from tree cover and with few exceptions the immediate surroundings had a rural feel to them, even though suburbia was visible only a short way off. The rest of the journey is going to be very different.

Putney and Wandsworth

In a matter of moments my riverside environment has been shot to pieces. It happened that quickly. A few minutes ago I was walking among the trees, and now I am dodging in and out of seemingly half of the world population as I elbow my way down Putney High Street. Rescue is at hand because instead of continuing through this teeming throng the pathway darts quickly to the left and loops around the churchyard of St Mary the Virgin and back to the river. Phew! That was close. The distance could not have been more than 100 yards but it took me into a nightmare world and then back out again. I am back to my river and with some relief step off again.

But what is this? No, no, no! This can't be right. After a short tantalizing glimpse of sanctuary the path diverts back onto the streets and deposits me in Deodar Road. Where did they get that name from? The Deodar is a type of cedar tree found in the western Himalaya regions of Afghanistan, Pakistan and Kashmir. It is known for its beauty, unlike its namesake road. Roy Plumley, of "Desert Island Discs" fame, used to live here. I too feel as though I have been marooned, without my choice of discs, and await rescue from my suburban isolation.

My prayers are soon answered. I am in Wandsworth Park, a haven of green among a brick-faced hell-hole. But it is a brief respite; the Gods are toying with me, bringing me up only to pull away and let me plunge deeper into the blackness. I am spat out onto a road that looks as though it is taking me into an industrial estate. With a superb irony this thoroughfare goes by the name of Point Pleasant.

Oh it gets worse. Have you ever noticed the names that developers give to the roads on industrial estates? There must be a management-speak thesaurus that they all use, and with some sort of inverse proportion to the businesses carried out in them. So I just knew that "Enterprise Way" would contain all the usual tatty works units with bits of cardboard boxes covering their forecourts. I am not disappointed.

A footbridge takes me over the River Wandle that gives rise to the name of the borough I am now in, Wandsworth. Straight after the footbridge the gods finally dump me at the bottom of the pit. They have lead me to the rubbish tip. A huge waste transfer station where all of the rubbish is taken by lorry to be transferred onto barges that take it to its final resting place. No doubt on to landfill somewhere in the estuary where it will be "out of sight – out of mind". It can not be denied that the sight of huge containers being lowered onto the barges has a type of morbid fascination. I even took a photograph to remind me later that this desecration of the riverside actually existed. This must be the lowest point of the whole walk.

Less than 24 hours later I was to be proved very wrong.

Within another few yards I change again from rags to riches. I am standing at St Nicholas Wharf, a magnificent new development of apartments with shops and piazzas with riverside promenade frontage. Unfortunately the next stretch of the pathway is going to be a lot of hassle. The entire waterfront is in various stages of development all the way between here and Albert Bridge. It is a case of threading between different developments that are in various stages of completion, sometimes walking along the riverside promenade but more often than not along the inland streets with the riverside buildings covered with scaffolding and protective coverings.

Gaudy signs tell me that my life will be so much better if I buy one of these dwellings. I would be in with the "In-Crowd". With the benefit of hindsight I can now say that I would also have been in severe negative equity.

Albert Bridge is one of the prettiest of the London bridges. Designed by Rowland Mason Ordish, it was first opened in 1872, but from its very earliest days there were questions against its sturdiness. After only 11 years it was strengthened by Sir Joseph Bazalgette, the designer of Putney Bridge. The bridge was further strengthened by the addition of a central pier in 1970's but concerns about its strength still prevail. There is even a rather quaint notice ordering all soldiers to break step when crossing the bridge in an attempt to prevent vibration damage to the structure.

Battersea Park

From Albert Bridge it is but a few steps into Battersea Park, and the building sites and rubbish tips of the last hour are forgotten in this 200 acre oasis in the midst of the city.

Two hundred years ago this area was known as Battersea Fields and was a well-known venue for a spot of dueling. I found a story that on 21st

March 1829 the Earl of Winchelsea and the Duke of Wellington came here to settle a matter of honour. It seems that having both turned up they decided that honour was satisfied. Wellington deliberately missed and then Winchelsea responded in the same manner. Both men apologised to the other and went on their separate ways.

Battersea Park was the home ground of "The Wanderers", who won the first ever F.A.Cup in 1872, beating the Royal Engineers 1-0. (Trivia; don't believe that sharp practice and skulduggery are unique to today's footballers. The winning goal was scored by Morton Betts, who was playing under the assumed name of A.H. Chequer who was clearly the first ringer to win an FA Medal; beat that Motty!).

The park was also the venue for the first game of football to be played under FA rules. This was an exhibition game held on 9th January 1864. Before then it seemed that each club played to its own rules, something that some of today's team managers believe should still be the case, obviously their own interpretation being the one that is used.

Battersea had interesting beginnings. Like so many things we have today it came about not because it was something that the people wanted, but because somebody else wanted to regulate what everybody else could do, and do a bit of "social engineering". As we shall see, Battersea was used many times in its 150 years for this.

During the 1830's public parks were considered as a means of improving public health, by providing open spaces away from the overcrowded and disease-ridden slums that were growing up as a result of the industrial evolution. Parks were also seen as a way of regulating behaviour and morals, and encouraging respect for Queen, Country and Empire.

The first designs for the park were drawn by James Pennethorne in 1845. Pennethorne was something of a parks specialist, being also involved in the designs for Regents Park, Kennington Park and Victoria Park. The original landscaping utilised the excavated material from the Surrey Docks to build up the ground. The carriageways and lake were added in 1854 by the first park superintendent, John Gibson. Gibson introduced trees and shrubs from around the world, creating in the process a rich landscape incorporating space and shape that was greatly admired. The work was completed in 1858 with the grand opening by Queen Victoria. The park became highly popular and was a destination for all levels of society.

The war years saw the park utilised for anti-aircraft batteries and barrage balloons. Large areas of the gardens were given over to allotments for the growing of vegetables. Another area was used as a pig farm.

Following the austerity of the war years, the government planned the Festival of Britain to demonstrate an optimistic future to the population. The South Bank area was to be the main focus for culture, and I will be walking that stretch tomorrow. Here at Battersea the focus would be on entertainment for the masses. Thirty seven acres of the park were devoted to the Battersea Pleasure Gardens in 1951. This was originally a temporary plan, but the huge popularity of the attractions kept the funfair going until its closure in 1974.

Wandsworth Council took over the management of the park in 1986, and with the support of funding from the European Union and the Heritage Lottery Fund have restored it to its former glory.

The park is certainly pleasant, and on this sunny spring day is being well used. To my right there is another surprise. What is that doing here?

An oriental monument, right in the middle of Battersea Park.

Standing at over one hundred feet high, this is the London Peace Pagoda. Gilded statues of Buddha look out over the park, and wind chimes tinkle in the air. It was built by the Nipponzan Myohoji Buddhist Order with assistance from the Greater London Council to celebrate the GLC Year of Peace in 1985. The Pagoda is one of many around the world dedicated to the promotion of world peace. In fact it was the seventieth to be completed. There is another one in England in, of all places, Milton Keynes.

The first Peace Temples were built in Hiroshima and Nagasaki. The original driver for these was a Buddhist Monk by the name of Nichidatsu Fujii (1885 – 1985) the founder of the Nipponzan Myohoji Buddhist Order. He had met and was inspired by Mahatma Gandhi in 1931, and in 1947 began instructing his followers to erect Peace Temples to promote peace throughout the world. The Temple is currently under the supervision of Rev Gyoro Nagase who was one of the volunteers who constructed the Temple.

The end of the park comes too soon, and it is time to leave the river again for yet another detour. This time it is around one of the most recognisable outlines in London, the derelict building that was once Battersea Power Station.

Battersea Power Station

So what do red telephone boxes, Liverpool Anglican Cathedral and the Tate Modern gallery have in common? They were all originally designed by Sir Giles Gilbert Scott (1880-1860), a noted architect and designer. The sad comparison is that Battersea now stands derelict and unused, while his other major power station, Bankside, has been transformed into the magnificent Tate Modern building, which I will be passing tomorrow.

The first parts of this building were started in 1929 and when it was finally opened in 1939 it was the largest brick-built building in the world. Battersea also proudly possessed the largest steam turbine in Europe, with a generating capacity of 105 Mega Watts. Soon after the war the capacity was increased to 500MW and the power station enjoyed its hey-day.

Progress rolls inexorably forward and soon newer power stations were opening that generated more efficient power and at considerably lower running costs. Battersea was rapidly becoming a liability. Station A became redundant in 1975, and the last electricity was generated from Station B in 1983.

For some people of a certain age the image of Battersea Power Station will be forever imprinted on their minds with a giant inflatable pink pig floating above the four chimneys. This was the famous LP cover for the Pink Floyd album "Animals" released in 1977. They had some real fun and games shooting this, because on the second day of shooting the inflatable pig broke free from its moorings and caused havoc with the Heathrow air traffic control system until it finally came to earth again in a field somewhere in Kent.

There are currently several different ideas of what could be done with the building, including developing it as a technology centre, but now it stands forlornly by the side of the Thames, waiting for new occupants to bring it back to life.

The detour is another trudge around the noisy, dusty streets of Nine Elms, apparently named because at one time there were nine glorious elm trees that graced the area. Now the only thing that gives any benefit whatsoever is a well placed Tesco Express that sells refreshing cans of pop, of which one is quickly downed to ease the spirit through the grim surroundings.

Prince of Wales Drive is the rather grand name for the road running past the power station. It also runs past the famous Battersea Dogs Home, and a few yaps can be heard as I pass by. There is something very strange about the pavement. There is a marked cycle lane upon it. All very well, but when the cycle lane approaches a lamp post it swerves around it, reducing the pedestrian walkway by half, but keeping the cycle lane. So to stop the local lycra-louts from smashing into a cast iron lamp post Wandsworth Council sends them into the pedestrians instead. Where do they find these people?

Just before Vauxhall Bridge there is another of those rare delights that sit in an otherwise dull surround. A relief-sculpture shows Father Thames wrestling with serpents and an octopus. The sculpture is by Stephen Duncan and provides a welcome lighter note as I approach the bridge.

Vauxhall Bridge

The pathway eventually emerges at Vauxhall Bridge, at first sight not the most spectacular of London's crossings. It is a steel-arched bridge opened in 1906, which replaced a previous cast-iron bridge which had proved incapable of supporting the traffic levels of the time. It would never have stood a chance with the traffic flows of today.

A closer look reveals that there are some interesting features on this bridge. Looking over the waters are bronze statues positioned on the abutments of the bridge. There are eight in all, four facing upstream and four facing downstream. They are all female, and depict the arts and sciences. The four facing upstream depict agriculture, architecture, engineering and pottery, while the four facing downstream represent government, education, fine art and astronomy.

The name "Vauxhall" given to the surrounding area is derived from "Faulkes Hall", the home of Faulkes de Breaute in 1200.

I cross the road at the bridge and notice that there are security men everywhere. Not surprising really because this is 85 Albert Embankment, officially known as the SIS building, but everyone knows that it is the headquarters of MI6, the home of the real-life James Bonds. The external appearance looks as if it has been build of white and green Lego bricks. There is so much "muscle" around the perimeter that I instinctively know that I will never be allowed to see what the inside looks like.

James Bond fans will have seen the building featured in three films, "Goldeneye", "The World is not Enough" and "Die Another Day". Fans will also be amused that the domain name mi6.co.uk has been acquired by a James Bond fan club and not the security organisation. A bold piece of cyber-squatting.

The thought crosses my mind. "Why, if it is meant to be so secret does everyone know where it is?" Then the conspiracy theory takes over. Perhaps this is just a decoy. Tell everyone the funny-folk are in residence, pack the outside with security and then they will all think it is the real HQ. When Ivan breaks in all he will discover are corridors of empty rooms while all the time the real spies are holed up somewhere in the middle of Exmoor. On the other hand could it be the ultimate "in-yer-face" macho statement. We are here. Come and have a go if you think you're hard enough. And nobody ever does.

Spies or no spies, the building provides a terraced walkway that is a welcome relief from the roadside walking from Battersea. It takes me along the Albert Embankment with a fine view across the river to the Tate Britain Gallery, and then under Lambeth Bridge to the start of one of the most popular tourist destinations of the entire Thames Pathway

Westminster

The view across the river is seen countless times every week on television. I have arrived at the Palace of Westminster

Before then let us take a look at the building behind me. Ignored by many of the sightseers it is an important palace in the history of England. Lambeth Palace has been the London residence of the Archbishop of Canterbury since the early 13th century. In fact, it was Stephen Langton who was the first Archbishop to take residence here. You will recall he was the Archbishop caught up in all the chicanery of King John and the Barons in 1215 resulting in the meeting to introduce Magna Carta.

The current resident is Dr.Rowan Williams, who leads a very different life to his earlier predecessors. In addition to his responsibilities as the senior Bishop of the Church of England, he also has the senior position of the Anglican Communion around the world.

The palace has been continuously developed over the years, and has had at least two major restoration projects. Firstly after the Civil War when it was almost destroyed by Cromwell's followers, and secondly following bomb damage during the blitz.

Next along is St Thomas' Hospital. And no, I have not put the apostrophe in the wrong place. It is meant to be plural, for the hospital is named after two St Thomases. They are St Thomas Becket and St Thomas the Apostle. The hospital was originally founded in Southwark by the monks of Southwark Priory, but moved to this present site in 1871.

I turn back to the major feature. How many people this afternoon are simply sitting on the seats and walls along this stretch of the promenade looking across the water at the familiar architecture. There must be several hundred. It is coming up to four o'clock in the afternoon and we are all waiting for one thing. We look expectantly towards the top of Clock Tower and wait.

The big hand moves to the vertical………

Dum,dum,dum,dum………..dah, dah, dah, dah………

Dum,dum,dum,dum………..dah, dah, dah, dah………

BONG !

BONG !

BONG !

BONG !

Not many people may know this, but (a) the bell is not the original, and (b) even the bell used now is not perfect.

The first bell was cast on 6th August 1856 by John Warner and Sons of Stockton-on-Tees. It weighed 16 imperial tons, (14.5 metric tonne). The commissioner of works for the new Palace of Westminster was Sir Benjamin Hall, and it is believed that the name "Big Ben" developed from his name.

While being tested, the bell cracked and was no longer able to be used. It was taken down and recast at the famous Whitechapel Bell Foundry on 10th April 1858 and came out as 13.76 tonne. The dimensions are 2.2metres tall, and 2.9metres diameter. It took eighteen hours to pull it up into position. It first chimed in July 1859, and in September guess what? Yes; it cracked again. Fingers were pointed, and in the end the hammer was blamed for being too heavy. The bell was twisted round so that a different part of the bell was struck, and the crack filled. It has worked perfectly well ever since, even if the tone is very slightly off-key. Another one for the trivia buffs, the bell strikes the pitch of "A".

There are also four "Quarter Bells" in the tower. These bells provide the chimes, and are tuned to the pitch of G sharp; F sharp; E and B. The sequence is known as the Cambridge chimes and is supposedly a variation on a phrase from Handel's Messiah. There are even words to the chime, derived from Psalm 37,

"All through this hour,

Lord be my guide,

And by Thy power,

No foot shall slide".

The clock is also fascinating. The clock and dials were designed by Augustus Pugin (1812 – 1852). Pugin was a brilliant designer particularly of ecclesiastical buildings. He is a particularly sad case. He died without seeing his work at Westminster completed. His descent into madness culminated in an early death at the young age of just forty years.

The clock faces are 23 feet (7m) in diameter, each supporting 312 pieces of opaque glass. The perimeter of the dials is gilded. At the base of each clock face is the inscription "Domine salvam fac Reginam nostrum Victoriam Primam", which translates as "O Lord keep safe our Queen Victoria the First.".

The hour hand is 9 ft (2.7m) long, and the minute hand is 14 ft (4.3m) long. The pendulum is 3.9m long, weighs 300Kg and beats once every 2 seconds. Cast your mind back to those old school physics lessons, measuring the swing of a pendulum. You may remember that the time of the swing is a function of the length of the pendulum and the weight of the pendulum. The guardians of the clock devised an ingenious but simple way of correcting the pendulum. They use a pile of old penny pieces and add or remove them from the base of the pendulum. Adding or removing a penny will change the speed of the clock by 0.4 of a second per day. This is how they keep the clock to such perfect time.

Not quite so ingenious is the winding gear. For all modern technology it still requires winding up by hand three times per week, which takes about one hour each time.

The chimes of Big Ben have rung out across the area, and we can all get up and continue on our way.

Some more quiz trivia. What are the colours of Lambeth and Westminster Bridges, and why? Well, the Palace of Westminster sits between the two bridges, and Lambeth Bridge is predominantly red to represent the covering on the benches in the House of Lords, and Westminster Bridge is mainly green to represent the colour of the benches in the House of Commons.

Westminster Bridge marks the end of the penultimate day. I stop in the middle of the bridge to look back at my path and reflect on the day. It has been a day of highs and lows, starting with the greenery of Richmond and Kew, the romance of the boat race stretch, the descent into the streets of Putney, rising up again to the huge glitzy modern developments signalling a bright future, down again to the waste transfer station, then back up again to the spiritual atmosphere of the Peace Temple before descending to the desolation of Battersea Power Station and then finally being uplifted by the glorious neo-Gothic Palace of Westminster and the unmistakeable chimes of Big Ben.

What would tomorrow bring?

DAY TWELVE

PART ONE

WESTMINSTER TO TOWER BRIDGE

1.6 Miles

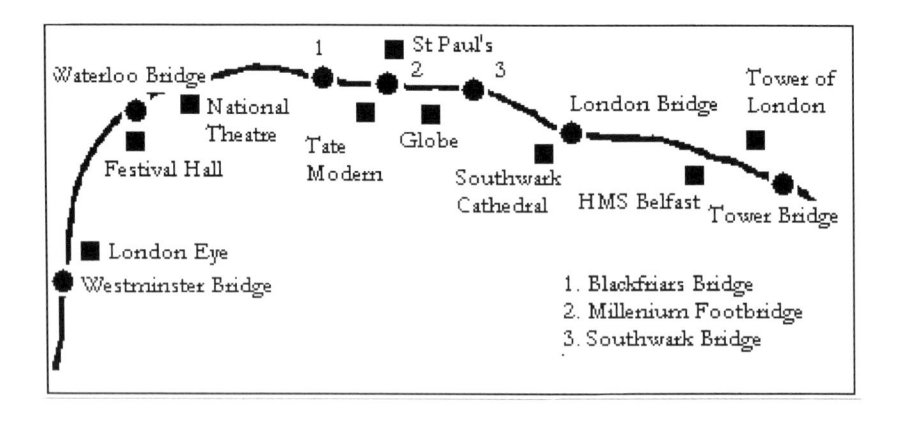

1. Blackfriars Bridge
2. Millenium Footbridge
3. Southwark Bridge

The Big Wheel

What a daft idea they muttered; total waste of money. How all the commentators poured scorn on the most ridiculous thing anybody had ever suggested to celebrate the millennium. It was doomed to failure from the start. Mark my words.

It is now the United Kingdoms most popular paying tourist attraction with over three and a half million visitors per year. Standing proudly at 443 feet high, (135m) with a circumference of 1,392 ft (424m) it has become an image synonymous with modern Britain. I have reached the wonder of design and engineering that is the London Eye.

Yes, it may have been a pretentious project to begin with. Full of arty-farty pseudo-waffle about how a wheel would represent the turning of the years of the millennium. But when it was completed everyone took it to their hearts and instantly fell in love with it.

This morning it is only just after 9am and the queues are already forming. The first passengers will not be able to board for almost another hour. Such is the popularity of this attraction. On a clear day you can see as far as Windsor Castle, 25 miles (40Km) away.

Everywhere along the promenade people are craning their necks, peering upwards at the spokes and hub. Cameras whir as would-be David Baileys all attempt to capture the ultimate image of sun glinting on steel spokes.

The inspiration for the eye came from husband and wife designers David Marks and Julia Barfield. The original sponsors were British Airways who saw the commercial potential of being associated with the project, and they retained a share of the ownership until early in 2008. The

London Eye is now owned and operated by the London Eye Company, a division of the Merlin Entertainments Group.

Since opening in March 2000 the Eye has won more than 75 awards for design, engineering and tourism. At the time of opening it was the largest ferris wheel in the world.

A single rotation takes 30 minutes, at a perimeter speed of 26cm per second. There are 32 capsules, each weighing 10 tonnes with a capacity of 25 people, enabling the wheel to carry 800 people per single revolution. Allegedly there are 32 capsules because there are 32 Boroughs of London. Whether that was arrived at by coincidence or design I am not sure, but it makes a nice story nonetheless.

The spindle and hub weigh 330 tones, making it more than twenty times the weight of Big Ben on the opposite side of the water. Quite amazingly, considering the dire reputation of the cars made by the same company in the late 20th century, the spindle and hub were manufactured in the Czech Republic by Skoda.

The combined weight of the wheel and capsules is 2,100 tonnes, so you can imagine that some very solid foundations are required to keep it all up. Underneath the A-frame support are 2,200 tonnes of concrete and 44 concrete pillars sunk to a depth of 33 metres each.

All in all a wonder of modern Britain. It took seven years of planning, designing and construction to bring it to life. Long may it remain to bring us joy.

The South Bank

Further along Jubilee Gardens the scene turns to street theatre. The inevitable human statues clad entirely in silver or gold. A gold king and queen, a silver Georgian gentleman and a guitarist completely covered in blue, who plays a little tune every time somebody drops a coin into his tribute box. A magician is starting to attract a crowd with a glass ball moving up and down in mid-air accompanied by some humorous patter to keep the punters interested. Only a few yards further down a breakdancer is boosting up his ghetto-blaster to provide a little competition, while opposite sits a juggler surrounded by all kinds of strange objects that he will soon be tossing into the air while everyone watches in the anticipation of them clattering to the floor, which of course never happens.

Beneath Hungerford Bridge two pavement artists are drawing out the first outlines of their picture for the day, and a caricaturist is setting up ready to turn the client's slightly prominent nose into a huge proboscis so that they can display their sense of humour to all of their friends by pinning up the finished sketch on their kitchen wall.

This is the South Bank, artistic quarter of London. The purpose of the buildings may be artistic, but the buildings themselves are certainly not. The largest concrete monstrosity is the Festival Hall, built for the 1951 Festival of Britain. The stark concrete does not do it any favours, but I have to remember that this was built in a more austere time. The whole area was cleared after the end of the war to provide a cultural location to cheer everyone up after the grim years of hostilities. Still, I can not forgive them for demolishing a brewery to make space for this.

The other two halls of the South Bank Centre are the Queen Elizabeth Hall and the Hayward Gallery. The Hayward has simply got to be one of the most hideous examples of sixties architecture still standing. Enough said.

Underneath Waterloo Bridge there is a huge second-hand book market and the browsers are already working their way through the boxes of books stacked along the trestles.

Another statue on a plinth blocks my way with an arm extended pointing towards the entrance of the building. This one is not human, it is a proper statue. It is of Sir Laurence Olivier playing Hamlet, and he is pointing towards the National Theatre.

The National Theatre moved here in 1976 and consists of three theatres, the large open-stage Olivier, the conventionally designed Lyttelton and a small studio theatre the Cottesloe. In truth this building is no better than its upstream companions despite improvements from the Lottery Fund.

Gabriel's Wharf

Gabriel's Wharf is a complete contrast. A square set back from the river, next to the old warehouse wall, it offers a welcome delight compared to the previous concrete monsters.

A bandstand occupies the centre of the plaza, and the surrounding area is covered with café tables and chairs. All around the perimeter are small boutiques selling fashion, crafts and a wide assortment of eats and drinks.

The brightly coloured facades are all old garages that have had shop-fronts fitted to them, making ideal shops and studios. Closer inspection reveals that the upper storeys are not genuine, but paintings on the old warehouse wall. This imaginative use of the surrounds gives a more permanent appearance to the scene.

The square provides a welcome haven from the bustle and stark surrounds of the arts complex. Time to indulge in an excellent Panini and two cups of coffee while watching the world go by.

Gabriel's Wharf and the neighbouring OXO Tower are a mark of triumph for the little man over the developer. For centuries this area of the South Bank had been a marshy wasteland, but during the 19th century it became packed with cheap housing as people flocked to the capital from the countryside. The housing was generally poor, and it could be said that during the war the Luftwaffe made improvements by demolishing some of it. After the war the government cleared a lot more of it for the Festival of Britain, and developers put up some more unattractive offices. There were few jobs for the locals and the population crashed from 50,000 at its peak to less than 4,000.

In 1977 another developer wanted to build a huge hotel and yet more ugly offices. What housing was left would be cut off from the river. Something snapped. This was the proverbial last straw. It was the thing up with which the remaining residents would not put.

The residents formed the Coin Street Action Group. No hotel; no offices. What they wanted was affordable houses for local people, local shops, and they wanted their river back. They must have been a formidable group. In 1984 they formed the Coin Street Community Builders, bought the land and set about demolishing the hated offices, redesigning the Thames Walkway and laying out a riverside gardens. The park is named Bernie Spain Gardens, after Bernadette Spain one of the original Action Group members.

Not content with that they set about rebuilding the housing, and then took over the derelict OXO Tower and turned that into flats and designer boutiques, not to mention a fashionable restaurant on the top floor. There are now over 200 dwellings and 60 shops in the complex.

The OXO Tower is, in its own way, another triumph of ingenuity over authority. The building was originally a power station and constructed around 1900. It soon became outdated and was purchased by the Liebeg Extract of Meat Company, who owned the OXO brand. They wanted to display a big advertising sign, but the council refused permission. Then the architect, one Albert Moore, had a bright idea. What if he designed some decorative windows for the top of the tower? He could design two circular patterns one above the other and put a crossed design in the middle. Who could object to that? Nobody did, and when it was finished and the lights were switched on in a particular manner, (just at random, naturally) it just happened to display OXO to everyone who looked at it from across the river. Brilliant!

Doggett's Coat and Badge

Immediately before Blackfriars Bridge is a four-storey London Pub with an unusual name; "Doggett's Coat and Badge". Where have I seen that before on this walk? It was in Henley Rowing Museum.

Thomas Doggett was an actor and theatre manager. He was manager of both Drury Lane Theatre and Haymarket Theatre. In 1715 he fell overboard while crossing the river in a ferry near Embankment and was rescued by a young Waterman. In gratitude he organised a race for six young watermen who had recently completed their apprenticeships. Doggett was also a local Whig politician, and arranged the race for August 1st 1715 to celebrate the anniversary of the accession of George I. The prize was a red coat with a large silver badge depicting the Hanoverian Horse and the word "Liberty".

The race was between "The Swan" at London Bridge and "The Swan" at Chelsea, a distance of just over four and a half miles. The event has been held every year since and is the oldest annually held sporting event in the world. Not wanting to make it easy the race would be against the ebbing tide. The old-style heavy wherries that were used in those days required great effort to move against such tides, and the contest could last up to four hours in poor conditions.

When Doggett died in 1721 he left in his will money to buy the coat and badge for future years, and decreed that the event should be held on the 1st August forever. The money in the will was handed over to The Fishmongers Company to carry out his instructions. These days the rowers use modern skulls and the date has changed to July, but otherwise the contest continues as Thomas Doggett intended all those years ago.

The Wobbly Bridge

I have found one of the best photographic points in London. Standing at the top of the steps on the south side of the Millennium Bridge offers a full-on view of St Paul's Cathedral and by standing on the pathway a few yards downstream of the bridge I can capture an image of the bridge sweeping across the river towards the cathedral dome.

You may remember that this is the "Wobbly Bridge". It is the first London Bridge across the Thames since Tower Bridge was completed and was meant to provide a Millennium experience carrying the general public between the Tate Modern Gallery and St Paul's. It certainly provided an experience the first day it was open.

The bridge is a footbridge, and as such is narrow at only 13ft (4m) wide, with a total length of 1066 ft (325m). It is supported by two piers, and is very pleasing to look at, and as I have already pointed out, makes an excellent subject for a photograph.

In theory the bridge can carry up to 5000 people, and when it was finally opened on June 10th 2000 everyone flocked to cross over it. Imagine their surprise when it moved under their feet.

Synchronous Lateral Excitation is the scientific name for this phenomenon. In simple terms what happened is that the vibrations of all of the people walking across the bridge sets off small vibrations that make the bridge sway ever so slightly. Reflex actions by the people walking on the bridge make them sway very slightly in sympathy to keep their balance, causing the bridge in turn to sway just a little bit more. Multiply this many times over and before you know where you are the bridge is swaying back and forth and everyone is behaving like Indiana Jones crossing an Amazonian ravine.

Naturally as soon as word got around everybody wanted to have a go. After all, you pay two quid to go on something similar at the fairground and this "ride" was free. Unfortunately "Health and Safety" soon put a stop to the fun and the bridge was closed on June 12th to make it safer.

It was finally opened again after much structural testing and correction, but it was not nearly so much fun. I walk across to St Paul's and back again just in case the bridge fancied returning to its erratic ways, but it remained motionless much to my disappointment.

The Tate Modern Gallery

At the southern end of the Millennium Bridge sits the Tate Modern Gallery. If you remember further back upstream we looked at Battersea Power Station in a state of dereliction and decay. This, too, is an old power station, coincidentally also originally designed by Sir Giles Gilbert Scott, but there the comparisons must cease.

This building has been magically transformed, and whilst the outside still has most of the original appearance, the inside is a wonder of design and a lesson in how to utilise light and space to stunning effect. It was opened in 2000, and stands as a credit to the imaginative redevelopment of some of our old buildings.

It is easy to take the mickey out of modern art so I shall not attempt to here. What is astonishing is that the Tate Modern is so incredibly popular. Current visitor rates are over five million for each of the last two years, and just looking around this morning there are plenty of people about. It is one of the top three tourist attractions in Britain and the bustling pavements surrounding the gallery give this statistic every support.

So popular is the gallery that an extension is planned at a cost of £215 million. The futuristic design will sit behind the existing building and will be open in time for the 2012 Olympic Games. To my mind the intended structure resembles a couple of giant triangular sandwich packs; but what do I know?

Shakespeare's Globe

The walk along the South Bank is slow, and is taking far more time than I have planned. This is because every few steps there is something else to stop and take a look at, unlike the upper reaches where I could keep up a good pace with the scenery changing very slowly.

Having only just got started again after the Tate Modern I have to stop to admire The Globe. To be strictly correct this is known as Shakespeare's Globe to avoid confusing it with the original Globe Theatre.

Back in Shakespeare's day the City Corporation did not approve of popular entertainment, and many of the theatres and bear-baiting rings crossed the river to the Bankside area of Southwark in order to continue their trade. Inevitably other entertainment trades sprung up as well, and the area was notorious for its bawdy revelry with numerous taverns and brothels. I was delighted during my researches to discover that most of these houses of ill repute were on land owned and controlled by the Bishop of Winchester whose palace was just around the corner from where I am standing. It puts a whole new slant on stories about the actress and the bishop.

Anyway, back to the story. The impresario of the day was Richard Burbage, who owned the number one venue of the day, under the highly imaginative name of "The Theatre". Burbage had a dispute with his landlord and this went unresolved for some time. Following Burbage's death in 1597, his two sons, Cuthbert and Richard decided enough was enough. They sold shares in a new company to four of their actors, including a certain Mr William Shakespeare, and then the whole company dismantled "The Theatre" and carried the timbers to Southwark where they built it back up again and called it "The Globe".

The Globe opened in 1599 and was used for most of Shakespeare's plays. The end came rather suddenly in 1613 during a performance of Henry VIII when a spark from a stage cannon set the thatched roof alight and the theatre burned to the ground in less than two hours. It was rebuilt, this time with a tiled roof, and continued to be a top location until it was closed by the Puritans in 1642. The Globe was demolished in 1644.

Nobody exactly knows what "The Globe" looked like. In fact, the only guidelines we have of any theatre design of the period are a few lines in some of the plays written at the time (Shakespeare describes his theatre as a "wooden O" in Henry V), and a couple of sketches.

Fast forward to 1949 when the American actor and director Sam Wannamaker visited London. He was disappointed to find that the Globe Theatre did not exist, nor was there anywhere else in London for Shakespeare's plays to be performed in the surroundings for which they were originally written. After several years canvassing his ideas to plug this gap he founded the Shakespeare's Globe Trust in 1970 and set about researching, designing and fund-raising for a reconstructed Globe to be built. It was 1987 before the first work started on clearing the ground and construction had only just been started in 1973 when Sam Wannamaker passed away.

Wannamaker's aim was to reconstruct the theatre as authentically as possible. This even included creating a thatched roof. It is claimed that this is the first thatched roof in the centre of London since the Great Fire. Modern fire resistant treatments have been used to take every precaution against the reconstruction suffering the same fate as the original building. The reconstructed theatre was opened by Her Majesty the Queen in June 1997.

Shakespeare's Globe is as close as we are ever likely to get to the original performances as The Bard intended. The Trust promotes education and research as well as putting on performances. There are daily workshops and lectures as well as a fascinating tour of the replica theatre which is highly recommended.

St. Marie Overie

Shortly after The Globe the pathway turns at the Anchor pub, where Samuel Pepys watched the Great Fire of London rage on the opposite bank, and then dives under a dark railway bridge to take me into the narrow, dark, dismal and alley-like Clink Street. A gibbet hangs from a corner wall with its decaying remains displayed as a deterrent to all who pass this way.

A sign on the wall announces that I am looking at the Clink Museum. The museum is not the original Clink, that is long gone, but a venue adapted from an old warehouse that sits on the original site. The area was known by the tautologous name of "Liberty of the Clink". The clink was a notoriously grim prison. Initially built in the 12th century to lock away religious non-conformists, it became a convenient place to incarcerate all those who caused breaches of the peace in the taverns and brothels of Bankside during its heyday. Once Oliver Cromwell had closed down all of the entertainments it was no longer required for this purpose, and became a debtors prison until it was burned down during the Gordon Riots of 1780.

I still can not help but shiver as I pass this dire stretch, and I am quickly standing at a plaque telling me that this piece of wall and window is all that remains of Winchester Palace. This was the home of the aforementioned Bishop of Winchester, landlord of the bawdy-houses of Elizabethan times.

The street leads me to St Marie Overie Dock where there is a full-sized reconstruction of Sir Francis Drake's ship, "The Golden Hinde". It is amazing to realise that Drake sailed around the world in a ship of this diminutive size. How did he manage to pack all of the necessary crew and supplies on to such a small vessel?

Southwark Cathedral

A couple of more sharp turns of the street and I am at Southwark Cathedral. If you try and name as many Cathedrals as you can I bet it is a long time before you think of Southwark, if at all. Not surprising, because it has only been a cathedral for a relatively short time, and has one of the smallest diocese. However, due to its location it is ideally situated to serve a much wider flock than those who live in its immediate parish.

A convent was believed to have been established here around the year 606, and St Swithun, Bishop of Winchester, is believed to have set up a college of priests sometime around 860. That gives us a connection with Winchester at least. The first actual reference comes in the Domesday Book, where a monastery is listed as having its own wharf for the unloading of goods.

In 1106 two knights, William Port de L'Arche and William Dauncey set up a new church that they dedicated to St Mary Overie and also founded an Augustinian Priory to administer to the sick and needy. They dedicated the hospital to St Thomas of Canterbury, and this eventually developed into St Thomas' Hospital at Lambeth Bridge.

Henry of Blois built Winchester Palace just a few minutes walk away, and the church remained under the influence of the Bishop of Winchester until the end of the nineteenth century.

In 1212 the priory, church and hospital were severely damaged by fire and work started to rebuild in the Gothic style. The church was continually expanded over the next three hundred years, and after the dissolution of the monasteries became the parish church of St Saviour.

Following the dissolution some parts of the monastery buildings were used for all sorts of things. One part was let out for a bakery, another as a pottery and a part was even used for keeping pigs!

The Church of St Saviour was in prime location for use by the entertainers of Bankside, and many of the names that appear on Shakespeare's First Folio also appear in the church registers. There is a further connection to Shakespeare in that his brother, Edmund, was buried here in 1607.

During the early 1800s the church faced two threats. The reconstruction of the medieval London Bridge would come within a few yards of the buildings, and the buildings themselves were becoming in a poor state of repair and spent some time without a roof. There was a move to pull the church down, but restoration won the day and the buildings were saved. No sooner was this accomplished than the London, Dover and Chatham Railway Company built a great eyesore of a viaduct right next to the restored church.

With all of this going on it was becoming more difficult for the cathedral at Winchester to support a church in South London. After a short experiment with transferring authority to Rochester, the Diocese of Southwark was formed by Act of Parliament and the cathedral came into being, with the rather grand name of Cathedral and Collegiate Church of St Saviour and St Mary Overie.

There we have Southwark Cathedral, and with a few more twists of the narrow London streets I arrive at London Bridge.

London Bridge

This is not the London Bridge whose construction caused the problems for the church of St Saviour. That one was built by John Rennie in 1825, but by the 1960's it was desperately in need of replacement. In 1967 Councillor Ivan Luckin had the bright idea of selling the bridge to help fund its replacement. Who would buy a bridge? Fans of Dragons Den will now imagine a Scottish accent loudly declaring "Ahm oot". But as the great "Arfer" Daley would have said, there is always a punter if you look for them.

This time it was Robert P McCulloch, owner of McCulloch Oil, who purchased the bridge for Arizona. Hands up all those who believe that whatever was said to the contrary he thought he had purchased Tower Bridge. Anyway, in 1968 he paid $2,460,000 for it and put it back up in Lake Havas City, Arizona. There it spans a man-made canal and is the centrepiece of an English theme park. Incredibly it is Arizona's second most popular tourist attraction, and when number one spot is taken by the Grand Canyon you can't get much better than that. I still think that Ivan Luckin puts "Del Boy" to shame.

While John Rennie's bridge sits in retirement in Arizona, what of its predecessors?

The first bridge would seem to have been a Roman military bridge built around AD 50. This would have been a wooden pontoon construction. The Britons built settlements at either end, the northern one being named Londinium. This early settlement was destroyed by Queen Boudicca and her chariots in AD 60, and then rebuilt by the Romans.

After the Romans left our shores the bridge seemed to be largely abandoned, with the river becoming a territorial boundary between the Kingdoms of Mercia and Wessex. The next account of a bridge at

London is a Saxon bridge put in place by Aethelred in 990. There then followed several centuries where the bridge would be up, then down, then built up again only to be down again, which probably gave rise to the nursery rhyme "London Bridge is Falling Down".

The first of the destruction was by Prince Olaf of Norway, who tore it down as a means of isolating the Viking inhabitants in 1014. It was obviously quickly rebuilt because there is reference to it being an obstruction for King Cnut as he made his way up the Thames in 1016.

A great storm in 1091 and the bridge was down again. The bridge was rebuilt and then destroyed by fire in 1136. What happened in the next forty years is unclear, but in 1176 it was decided to build a new bridge with stone. This took thirty three years to complete, but by 1209 King John was the proud owner of the lowest crossing of the river. We have met John before, and if he could make a few groats out of it he would. John sold licences for people to run businesses on the bridge and it soon developed into a ramshackle affair of narrow shops and workshops crammed on to the bridge.

In 1212 there was a fire which caused severe damage at the Southwark end. Simultaneously there was another fire at the northern end, and many hundreds of people were trapped in the middle and perished.

The stone bridge existed for over 600 years, but it was rather like "Trigger's Broom"*. Parts were continually falling away and had to be replaced. The bridge was a long series of small arches, which would have caused something of a barrier to the flowing waters. In fact there are estimates that there could have been as much as six feet difference between the upstream and downstream water levels, with dangerous rapids and currents that would pull away at the bridge supports.

* ("Trigger's Broom"; In an episode of "Only Fools and Horses" council road-sweeper Trigger claims that he had used the same broom for 20 years, and then goes on to say that during that time it had been fitted with 17 new heads and 14 new handles.)

There were gateways at each end of the bridge, and the southern gateway, known as "Stone Gateway" was notorious for its grisly display of traitors' heads. The traitor would have their head cut off, dipped in tar to make it resilient to the elements, and then displayed on a spike as a deterrent to others. The first head to be so displayed was that of William Wallace in 1305. The practice continued for 355 years, and among the most notable heads on display during this time were those of Jack Cade, Sir Thomas More and Thomas Cromwell. King Charles II put a stop to this custom when he was restored to the monarchy in 1660.

By the time we reach 1722 traffic over the bridge was so bad that it could take up to an hour to cross the bridge. The narrow gaps between the shops and houses meant that it only needed one cart to break down and everything stopped. The Lord Mayor decreed that in order to speed up the traffic flow travelers going north must keep to the west side, and those travelling south must keep to the east. Thus we have the first road traffic act decreeing that in Britain we will drive on the left.

The next key stage was the removal of the shops and houses. This clearance began in 1758 and took four years to complete. The bridge was now clear again, but by the early 19th century it was obvious that the bridge needed replacing. River traffic was severely impeded and the crossing traffic was as heavy as ever, leading to costly maintenance. A competition was organised to design a new bridge, which was won by John Rennie, which brings us back to this bridge being sold to Arizona.

H.M.S.Belfast

Under the bridge, turn left down a narrow alley and I am back to the riverside. After only a few steps I have arrived at HMS Belfast, the last of the heavy British Navy "Town Class" cruisers.

Cruisers were designed with the purpose of protecting commercial shipping, and when they were built HMS Belfast and her sister ship HMS Edinburgh were the largest and most powerful cruisers in the Royal Navy. HMS Edinburgh was sunk in May 1942, but Belfast survived the war and has been preserved for the nation, the first Royal Navy ship to be preserved since HMS Victory.

H.M.S.Belfast has been moored here as a museum ship since it was opened to the public on 21st October 1971, appropriately enough that date being Trafalgar Day. The vessel receives over 250,000 visitors per year, but many more I suspect spend time as I am doing now, leaning on the riverside rails admiring the ship with the Tower of London on the opposite bank serving as a spectacular backdrop.

The ship is now part of the Imperial War Museum and is open daily. During service the decks would have bustled with the activity of up to 850 men, but today it is swarming with schoolchildren out on a history lesson.

The ship was built at Harland and Wolff Shipyard in Belfast, and launched on 17th March 1938 by Mrs Neville Chamberlain, the Prime Minister's wife.

Specifications:

Displacement	11,553 tonnes
Length	613ft (187m)
Beam	69ft (21m)

Draught	19ft 6in (6.1m)
Armament	12 x six-inch guns
	8 x four-inch guns
	12 x Bofors Anti-aircraft guns
Maximum speed	32 knots
Propulsion	4 x Admiralty three-drum boilers
	4 x steam driven Parsons turbines
	4 x drive shafts generating 80,000 shaft horsepower
Complement	750 to 850

Following completion HMS Belfast was commissioned into the Royal Navy on 5th August 1939 under command of Captain G.A.Scott DSO RN.

HMS Belfast spent the first few weeks following the outbreak of the war on patrol out of the Cruiser base at Scapa Flow, (Orkney). The principal objective of the patrols was to cut off the German supply line to their ports, and on October 9th 1939 HMS Belfast successfully boarded and captured the SS Cap Norte.

The initial glorious success of Belfast came to an abrupt end only a month later when on 21st November the cruiser was severely damaged by a magnetic mine when coming out of the Firth of Forth. Although casualties were light there was severe damage to the hull and machinery and it would be almost three years before Belfast would be able to be repaired and resume active service.

Belfast came back to service in November 1942 considerably "beefed up" with the latest fire-power and technology and was soon back in the thick of the action, this time in the icy waters of the Arctic. The ship's mission this time was to keep open the supply routes to the northern Russian ports. These routes were essential in order to keep the Russian forces supplied for the Eastern Front, but the risk was extremely high. Up to half of a convoy could be sunk before reaching the safety of a port. During the operations the Merchant Navy lost over 30,000 men and over 5,000 ships keeping the Eastern Front supplied.

On December 26th 1943 the Belfast was a key player in one of the most significant sea battles of the North Atlantic. The Scharnhorst was one of Germany's largest battle cruisers and following an unsuccessful attack on a convoy was hit by a shell from HMS Norfolk that caused considerable damage. The German ship tried to regain port, but was pursued by HMS Belfast and HMS Sheffield who managed to drive the Scharnhorst into the guns of the waiting HMS York. The Scharnhorst was literally "dead in the water" and sank into the waters.

On D-Day the Belfast was a key part of the bombardment of the Normandy coast to protect the allied troops as they landed and made their way inland. Belfast gave support to the British and Canadian troops on "Gold" and "Juno" beaches for the first five weeks of the invasion.

Belfast was back in action for the Korean War giving support to British, American and South Korean forces until September 1952 when she returned to Britain.

The next few years were spent on routine patrols and exercises until finally HMS Belfast was signed off at Devonport on 24th August 1963. There followed a vigorous campaign to save the ship from the scrap-yard, and eventually in 1971 HMS Belfast arrived at her retirement home on the south bank of the River Thames.

The Tower of London

On the opposite bank sits the Tower of London. For centuries the White Tower dominated the London skyline. Today its ninety feet of height are insignificant against the city background.

The Tower was started by William the Conqueror as a fortress stronghold to keep down potential rebellion against the Norman Conquest. Since that time it has been added to and taken centre-stage of so many incidents during its history that it becomes a complete story in itself, far too great to do it full justice here.

Over two million people visit each year, and it is one of the "must-see" heritage attractions on the tourist trail. It houses the Crown Jewels, despite several attempts to spirit them away by various dubious characters. The most famous of these was Colonel Blood, whose attempt in 1671 to steal the collection resulted in the same failure as all those who went before him, as well as all those who tried to follow.

The Tower has also been used as a prison. The first prisoner was one Ranulf Flambard, erstwhile Bishop of Durham, who also became the first prisoner to escape. He accomplished this in comic-book hero style by climbing down a rope that had been smuggled up to him. That was back in 1101. Since then many of the famous and infamous have been incarcerated here over the centuries; the Princes in the Tower, (allegedly murdered by command of the future Richard III), Thomas Moore, Sir Walter Raleigh, Anne Boleyn, Lady Jane Gray, Guy Fawkes, Rudolf Hess and the Kray Twins.

Once upon a time the Tower of London and its resident "Beefeaters" were synonymous with the city itself, and were used as symbols to represent the capital. However, it is the next object of my attention that has in most peoples minds become the iconic image of London; the magnificent and instantly recognisable Tower Bridge

Tower Bridge

As London continually expanded during the eighteenth and nineteenth centuries the traffic pressures were becoming greater with every year that passed. The pressures in West London were alleviated with the building of many bridges, but below London Bridge there was nothing. A major obstacle was that any form of traditional bridge would restrict access to the Pool of London, the dockland area situated between London Bridge and the Tower of London. A committee was formed in 1876 to examine the possibilities of a bridge or subway solution, and they decided to put it out to public competition. Over fifty proposals were received and the winning one was submitted by Horace Jones, the City Architect, and his engineer Sir John Wolfe Barry. Their suggestion was for a "bascule" bridge, allowing it to open to allow ships to pass beneath. Work commenced in 1886 and the bridge was opened on 30th June 1894.

Let's look at some of the statistics. Total length of the bridge is 800 ft (244m), and each of the two towers stands 213 ft (65m) high. The central span is 200l(61m) wide. Each bascule weighs over 1,000tonnes and is lifted to an angle of 81 degrees. The upper walkway, designed so that pedestrians could cross while the bridge was raised stand 143 ft (44m) above the high water mark.

The mechanisms for lifting the bascules are in the base of each tower. Originally they were steam operated, but now use an electro-hydraulic system.

The construction is of steel, clad with granite and Portland stone, giving it a Gothic appearance that fits well with the nearby Tower of London. The steel was originally a chocolate-brown colour, but was repainted in red, white and blue for the Queens Silver Jubilee in 1977 and it has remained so ever since.

The Gherkin

The Tower of London is almost invisible in the London skyline. Looking across the water the eyes focus on the outline of one of London's newest and best loved buildings. Catch the sun at the right angle and it sparkles across the city.

The official address is 30 St Mary Axe; unofficially everyone calls it "The Gherkin". Why "Gherkin" took hold is something that is no doubt typical of the way certain names catch on with the English. A very witty suggestion was "The Crystal Phallus" but that got nowhere, so calling it after its first major occupant and naming it the "Swiss Re Tower" was a definite non-starter. Some wag somewhere in London must have said in typical Cockney fashion "Nah mate, looks like a gherkin to me, John" and the name stuck.

The Gherkin stands on the site of the old Baltic Exchange. After several attempts at obtaining permission for different designs to replace the old building in the City, it was finally decided to go for Lord Foster's spectacular symmetrical tower.

There are forty floors with an area of over half a million square feet. (516,100 sq ft, 47,950 sq metres). It reaches 591 ft (180m) into the sky, making it the sixth highest building in the capital. Its surface is covered with 24,000 square metres of glass, equivalent to five football pitches. Swedish contractors Skanska took three years to build it, and it was opened in May 2004.

Turning to face downstream from the bridge I can see London's tallest buildings that are going to dominate the skyline during the remainder of my walk, the skyscrapers of Canary Wharf.

DAY TWELVE (PART TWO)

TOWER BRIDGE TO THAMES FLOOD BARRIER

10.0 Miles

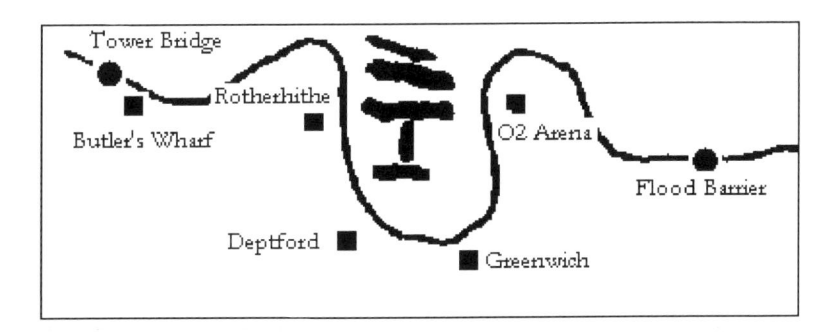

Butlers Wharf

When it was completed in 1871, Butler's Wharf was the largest docking and warehousing complex on the entire river. Its narrow cobbled streets now provide the first stages for my final leg of the walk. I have passed under Tower Bridge and am now looking down Shad Thames, a narrow street crossed by many small ironwork bridges. Shad Thames is a corruption of St John at Thames, which was derived from the Knights Templar who owned this area during medieval times.

The street is typical of the scene that we all imagine Dickensian London to have been like. I can visualise the smog swirling along the street and Bill Sykes slowly becoming visible as he approaches through it with his ill-gotten gains tucked away under his coat and his faithful dog "Bulls-eye" trotting at his heels. The location has been used for Dr Who, but one would have thought that with all of their technology the Daleks would have chosen a more attractive place to invade.

Only a short distance down the street the path takes a sudden left into an alleyway to take me to the river once again. The alleyway has the intriguing name of "Maggie Blake's Cause". Who was Maggie Blake, and what was her cause? I later discovered that Maggie Blake was a leading local activist during the period that the wharf was being redeveloped during the 1990's. Her "cause" was to ensure that the public would continue to enjoy access to the riverbank and be able to walk freely along the side of the Thames, and this alleyway to the river is the result of her efforts.

The riverside is packed with restaurants, and shortly I come across the Design Museum. The museum moved here in 1989 from its former home in the "Boiler House" at the Victoria and Albert Museum. The original design museum was instigated by Sir Terence Conran, who was also responsible for much of the modernising and development of Butler's Wharf. The museum is dedicated to contemporary design, and features fashion, vehicles, household objects and just about anything you can imagine, (plus some that you won't). Over 200,000 visitors a year come to admire the exhibits, and many students come to be inspired by the creations so that they can develop ideas of their own.

At the end of Butler's wharf is St.Saviour's Dock, or rather what is left of it. A footbridge takes me over the old dock entrance, avoiding the need to venture further inland. This area was once known as Jacob's Island, a notorious Victorian slum. One newspaper once described it as "the capital of cholera". Charles Dickens used this area to describe the filthy rookeries of London in "Oliver Twist". It is a lot better now, with new housing developments occupying the site of the former atrocities.

Dr.Albert Salter

After Cherry Garden Pier is another one of those surprises that the path throws up every now and again. A bronze statue of a man in a pork-pie hat sits on a bench, waving at his daughter, while the family cat sits on the riverside wall. This is a tribute by sculptor Diane Gorvin to Dr Albert Salter (1873 – 1945), doctor, politician and social reformer.

Albert Salter studied medicine at Guy's Hospital, and came to work among the poor of Bermondsey. The area was subject to poverty, employment mostly depending on casual labour at the docks. Albert decided that he was the one to do something about it and in 1903 was elected to Bermondsey Council. Together with his wife Ada, they set about improving the health and living conditions of their locality as best they could.

Salter stood as a Labour candidate for Bermondsey in 1922, was rejected at the 1923 election but returned again in 1924. He held the seat until he stood down at the 1945 election shortly before his death.

His daughter, Joyce, died aged nine with scarlet fever, and the sculpture shows the doctor remembering happy days with his daughter.

On the opposite side of the road are the last remains of Edward III's Manor House, built in 1353.

Rotherhithe

Now for another quiz question. Where did the "Mayflower" begin her journey to America? Correct; Rotherhithe.

The Mayflower pub stands on the site formerly occupied by The Shippe, and is said to mark the point where its namesake departed for the new colonies.

The captain and part-owner of "The Mayflower" was local man Christopher Jones, who is buried in the local churchyard of St.Mary's. The First Mate and also part-owner was another Rotherhithe man John Clarke, who gave his name to Clarkes Island, Plymouth Bay, Massachusetts. They set sail with their crew from Rotherhithe, and met up with the ship "Speedwell" at Southampton. The two ships picked up the Pilgrim Fathers at Plymouth, and on 6th September 1620 off they went. The Speedwell soon developed difficulties after springing a leak and eventually turned back, which is why people have only ever heard of the Mayflower. After landing in America on 21st December, the ship stayed with the Pilgrim Fathers until April, and then returned to England, docking at Rotherhithe in May.

A little further along there is a further reminder of the connection between Rotherhithe and the early settlers. The statue, "Sunbeam Weekly and the Pilgrim's Pocket" stands on the walkway at Cumberland Wharf. The work is by Peter McClean, depicting a newsboy in 1930's attire, reading a copy of the newspaper depicting the story of "The Mayflower" and all that has happened in the USA since those early days. The pilgrim is reading the paper over the boy's shoulder, looking astonished at how the world has developed since he landed at Plymouth Rock in 1620. The boy's dog also appears to be trying to read the newspaper, standing on its hind legs.

The path turns again into streets, and amazingly I walk past the Docklands Hilton. There are certain things in life that seem to fit the name, but a Hilton in this area is not one of them.

Another set of words that do not at first seem to fit together are Surrey, Docks and Farm. Incredible as it may seem, there is a two-acre farm right here in the middle of the reclaimed dock area. The farm was established in 1975, and its primary purpose is to educate and inform the people of the city about the farming that is so important for supplying the metropolis with its food requirements. On its two acres the farm keeps a variety of livestock, cows, pigs, goats, sheep and poultry. Vegetables and herbs are lovingly tended in their relevant gardens. There are bee hives, a milking parlour and a classroom where children from all over London come to learn about the mysteries of the countryside. More importantly for the benefit of my immediate needs there is a café.

The route continues with a succession of housing streets interspersed with short riverside walkways and a series of footbridges providing access over the many inlets from the main river.

Deptford

I pass the boundary stone marking the border between Rotherhithe and Deptford. If I had previously thought that some earlier stretches of the Thames Path were depressing it is only because I had not yet set foot in Deptford.

Deptford is derived from "Deep Ford" which relates from the ford across the River Ravensbourne at what is now Deptford Bridge, and is mentioned in Chaucer's "Canterbury Tales". It is one of the most densely populated areas of Britain. Unemployment is twice the national average and the crime rate is way above the national average.

Rather than going on about how grim it all is, let us look at some brighter things about the place.

Deptford was once a small fishing village. Then along came Henry VIII who turned it into a naval dockyard. It was the first Royal Dockyard and became famed throughout the world for its shipbuilding prowess. So famous was Deptford that in 1698 Peter the Great stayed here for three months so that he could study the science of shipbuilding. To commemorate this visit there is a statue of Peter the Great that stands proudly at Deptford Creek

Trinity House, the organisation that ensures safe navigation around Britain's shores was founded here in 1514. A group of mariners calling themselves "The Guild of the Most Glorious Trinity of Deptford" were granted a royal charter by Henry VIII. The name is derived from the church next to the original dockyard, the Holy Trinity of St Clement. The first Master of Trinity House was Sir Thomas Spurt, who at that time was also captain of the King's flagship, the "Mary Rose".

Sir Francis Drake, if we could talk with the great man today would have very fond memories of Deptford. It was here that he received his knighthood from Queen Elizabeth I. The ceremony took place on the deck of Drake's flagship the "Golden Hind".

The Elizabethan playwright Christopher Marlowe (1564 – 1593) came to Deptford, and probably wished he hadn't, because he was murdered. The felony allegedly took place in a house in Deptford Strand on 30th May 1593. There are several different versions of how exactly he died, and more intriguingly why. It is all very mysterious, and involved plots concerning religion, heresy and all sorts of jiggery-pokery. Some say the murder happened at a local inn with a dispute over the payment of a bill, others say it occurred in a house where Marlowe was meeting with some royal spies. Others say it was the work of an Elizabethan "hit-man" who was disposing of Marlowe before he could testify against a group of powerful and influential men who had been up to no good. Whatever the reason, Marlowe was stabbed and he died. His body was buried in the churchyard of St Nicholas Church at Deptford

Cutty Sark

Onwards to the Cutty Sark that provides such a notable landmark of the London Marathon. It is disappointing to find that today it is enclosed by boards and unable to be seen. This is because of the renovation project that commenced in 2006 and was originally planned to finish in 2009. A fire on 21st May 2007 put back the work schedule and it is now expected to open to the public again in spring 2010.

Cutty Sark is an interesting name for a ship. In the Scottish dialect a cutty sark is a short chemise, and was the nickname given to Nannie, a character who wore such a garment in Robbie Burns's poem "Tam

O'Shanter". To further connect the ship with the poem the figurehead on Cutty Sark was named Nannie.

The ship was designed for exploiting the tea trade. Premium prices were obtainable for the first tea brought to England from China each year, and speed of transportation was essential. Cutty Sark could achieve a speed of up to 17 knots, which was quite exceptional for the time. Eventually the tea clippers lost out to steamships that were not only more reliable, but they could also considerably shorten the journey by using the Suez Canal as a short-cut.

Cutty Sark was built for Captain John by Scott and Linton at Dumbarton, and was launched on November 22nd 1869. The displacement was 2,100 tonnes, with a hull of 212 ft in length and a beam of 36 ft. Fully laden the vessel had a draught of 21ft.

Willis sold the ship in 1895 to the Portuguese Company "Ferreira", who changed the name of the craft to their company name and sailed it under the flag of Portugal. . In 1916 Ferreira was dismasted off the Cape of Good Hope, and after rerigging was relaunched under the name "Maria do Amparo". In 1922 the ship was purchased by Captain William Dowman, who restored the original design and reverted to the original name. He used it for training purposes, and the ship was moored at Falmouth and Greenhithe before arriving at its final destination at Greenwich.

When the ship is unveiled to the public again in 2010 it will have been restored to its full former glory, and once again be the major feature along this part of the pathway.

Greenwich Naval College

The path next takes me on a narrow walkway in front of the Old Naval College. This baroque masterpiece was designed by Sir Christopher Wren and is one of the most magnificent structures in London. Originally the buildings were constructed for the purposes of a hospital, but now it is used by a variety of organisations under the controlling body of the Greenwich Foundation.

In a former time the site was that of the Palace of Placentia, more commonly known as the Greenwich Palace. It was reputed to be the favourite home of Henry VII and was the birthplace of Elizabeth I. The palace unfortunately fell into disrepair during the years of the Civil War, and was eventually demolished in 1694.

The idea for a Royal Hospital for Sailors on the site came from the then Queen, Mary II wife of William III. The idea soon gained momentum, and when Sir Christopher Wren and his assistant Nicholas Hawkesmoor volunteered their services free of charge as the architects of the building the project swiftly got under way. The Queen however was not so passionately in favour of the hospital that she would let it interfere with her view of the river from the Royal House. Wren had to design the buildings according to the Queen's wishes hence why there is a distinctive gap in the buildings that enabled the royals to continue to enjoy their view of the Thames from their residence.

The hospital took sixteen years to complete between 1696 and 1712, but when finished was a magnificent example of architecture. To be fully appreciated in all its splendour the building needs to be viewed from the opposite bank which can be reached by using the Greenwich foot tunnel.

The Hospital became established as a home for injured sailors, along similar lines to the Chelsea Hospital for injured and pensioned soldiers.

Greenwich pensioners wore distinctive blue uniforms in a similar way to the more well-known red of the Chelsea Pensioner. Many sailors benefited from the hospital, and the Greenwich Hospital Charity still exists to support seafarers and their dependants.

When the hospital closed in 1869 the buildings were adapted to become the home of the Greenwich Naval College teaching all of the new technologies that were required in the ever-changing Royal Navy. Thus it remained until the College moved to its present location at Shrivenham, near Swindon in 1998.

It is no surprise to find that the buildings are all Grade I listed to give maximum protection. The site today is administered under the direction of the Greenwich Foundation and a remarkably good job they are doing to make full use of the facilities. The University of Greenwich leases a large part of the buildings for educational use. The Trinity School of Music has also leased a considerable amount of space for its various melodic uses. In addition to all this the Greenwich Foundation open the grounds and information centre daily for the benefit of the general public.

Time

Before leaving this part of Greenwich it is time to talk about time.

The Greenwich Observatory was founded by Charles II in 1675. It was the first building in Britain to be purpose built for scientific research. The first Astronomer Royal was John Flamsteed.

The observatory was set up for a specific reason. In order that the ships of the English Navy would be able to exactly locate position on the ocean it was vital to measure longitude. This is not easy. Latitude was easy, it could be done by measuring the angle of the sun, but longitude was an entirely different matter. To measure longitude required knowing the time at a fixed meridian, and also the exact local time. For this reason ships carried two clocks, one set at a fixed time for a specific meridian and the other was changed as the ship moved. Quickly one moves into matters of definition, not least of which is where a fixed meridian should be, and what the time is at any instant on that meridian. It was first proposed that the meridian should be fixed at Greenwich in 1833.

A conference held in Washington DC in 1884 revealed that 72% of the world's shipping used Greenwich, and 28% used various others around the world. Again it was suggested that the best answer was Greenwich and nearly every nation agreed but one. Can you guess which one?

Inevitably it was the French. They wanted to use the well known maritime location of Paris. Anyone who has read "The Da Vinci Code" will know that there is a meridian line in Paris, and the French did not want to change it for Greenwich. They did offer to accept it on the condition that Britain adopted the metric system and gave up miles, but they did not expect us to agree. Although they bowed to the inevitable eventually, it was not until 1978 that they gave their official approval.

So Greenwich became the undisputed centre of time and the meridian is marked in several places around the borough.

There is a last piece of time that is worthy of note, the Greenwich Time Ball. This is situated on a pole at the top of the Flamsteed Building and has been used since 1833 to signal time to the ships on the river. Every day, at precisely 12.55 the bright red ball is raised to halfway up the mast. At 12.58 it is raised to the top, and at precisely 13.00 it is dropped to the base of the pole. It is lovely to see that in this digital age it is still in daily use.

North Greenwich and The Dome

Deptford has nothing on North Greenwich. Whatever depths I had been through were mere blips as the surroundings crashed to a new low. This was an industrial wasteland of the lowest order. Shoddy factory shells producing goodness knows what. Groups of depressed-looking people in shabby clothes with that unmistakeable look of the itinerant worker from some bedraggled and desperate country whose name always seems to end in –stan. There are notices everywhere warning "Danger – Keep Out", as if anyone in their right mind would be tempted to venture to break-in to seek treasures in these run-down wastelands. Strange smells fill the air, telling me that somewhere nearby there is a chemical works that would only be allowed to operate far from regular habitation.

Do you remember the old westerns where the town was completely deserted? The film director always seemed to show a ball of tumbleweed being blown down the main street. As I walk around the Millenium Dome I can not help but look for the familiar tumbleweed. The "Dome" was Tony Blair's great vision for the future of Britain and what a depressing place it is. If this is the result of rejuvenation then God help Stratford after the Olympics have been and gone. It is a truly desolate place.

The "Dome" itself still looks a very impressive building. Designed by award-winning architect Richard Rogers it is instantly recognisable. Built upon the meridian line it has twelve 100m high support towers, representing the twelve months of the year, (or some others claim it is the twelve numerals of the clock-face). The diameter is 365m, representing the days of the year.

It was not the building itself that was the problem, it was what was on the inside. Or to be more exact what wasn't. We were told that the dome was to hold "The Millenium Experience", which was so hyped-up and over promoted that it would have even embarrassed the great P.T.Barnham himself. What was eventually put on display was a load of pseudo-sociological nonsense. The popular press scented blood and indulged in a feeding frenzy. Amazingly the Millenium Experience was still the top tourist attraction for the year 2000 with over six million visitors.

However, what was not there were a further six million visitors. All of the finance had been calculated on the assumption that the Dome was capable of attracting twelve million people through its doors. This wild speculation over attendance figures caused the financial ruin of the whole project. When the exhibition was closed at the end of December 2000 there were not many tears shed.

The dome was purchased by the Anshutz Entertainment Group, who have redeveloped the building, and sold off the name to a telephone company so it is now officially known as "The O2 Arena". The main arena can seat 20,000 people for a concert, and there is a second hall, "Indigo2" that can accommodate 2,350. An eleven-screen cinema complex completes the facility.

So, we have the complete opposite of the year 2000. Then we had a fine building and surroundings with a load of tat inside, and now we have a marvelous inside with desolation outside.

The deserted landscape continues around the Greenwich peninsula, and then it is back to an industrial estate again. I trudge along past unit after unit representing the bottom-end of the automotive market, thinking to myself that it would have been far better to have finished my walk at Tower Bridge. Just as this low ebb was reached I came to the end of the shabby estate and before me lay the last wonder of my journey.

The Flood Barrier

From a distance it looks like a line of "hoodies" crossing the river. As I get closer the stainless steel hoods of one of the engineering marvels of the world become clearer. There in front of me is the end of my journey, the Thames Flood Barrier.

The dangers of a serious flood to London cannot be overstated. The workings of the capital would come to a complete stop and take many months to get going again. Adverse weather combined with certain tidal conditions would cause a tidal surge in the North Sea that would be magnified by the Thames Estuary and force a wall of water into the city. To prevent this potential devastation the Greater London Council commissioned the Flood Barrier.

Work started in 1974 and the barrier was officially opened on May 8th 1984. The defences have had to be used more than a hundred times since then to protect against possible flooding. The gates only need to be closed for high tide to stop the upward surge. When the tide is ebbing the gates can be opened to allow the flows from the upper reaches to enter the sea.

The barrier is a formidable piece of engineering, stretching for 572 yards from bank to bank. The steel cowls cover the lifting mechanisms and divide the river into manageable sections. Between each of the towers are the gates. When open the gates lie in concrete dishes parallel to the river bed, and are pivoted into an upright position when required to fulfil their purpose. The four largest gates are 61m wide and 20m high, each one weighing 3,500 tonnes. The two smaller navigation gates are 31m wide, and at each of the ends are two radial gates completing the bank to bank barrier.

Testing takes place every month, when the gates are raised into position. The dates are published on the Environment Agency website.

REFLECTIONS

It is an old cliché but still nonetheless true that a journey is a metaphor for life.

I lean on the railings and watch the waters flow past the cowls of the flood barrier and gain the freedom of the sea. The river has come to the end of its existence and enters into the vast eternity of the oceans.

It is difficult to drag myself away. The river holds me like a magnetic force as though Father Thames knows that our grip on each other is fading and as soon as I turn away the special relationship we have shared and enjoyed will be gone forever.

The memories of the last two weeks course through my head.

Today the sun is shining and the warmth of summer is almost here. To reach this point I have had to cope with the English weather in all its moods. I started off in sunshine, then it was rain, wind, more rain, glorious sunshine, yet more rain and finally the sun has come out again to give a welcome glow to the finale.

I have seen the Thames grow from a helpless little puddle growing through its infancy to become the dominating force of its surroundings. I have wondered at the beauty of the rapidly changing and maturing character of the middle reaches. The iconic image of Tower Bridge fixes itself like an oil painting, forever preserving the river at its peak. I have despaired at the desolation and neglect the great waterway has fallen into during its last few miles. I suspect that the river itself often looks back to its middle stages and wonders where the glory days have all gone.

Not at all like life then.

ACKNOWLEDGEMENTS

The details in this book have been collated from numerous snippets of information I have gathered together. These came from various sources including notices along the pathway, guide books and the internet. I have made efforts to double-check where possible, and apologise if there are any errors.

Thanks to my wife Norina who walked with me during the first and last days and provided transport to the various daily start and finish points where public transport was difficult.

Thanks to my son Owen who has built an accompanying website
www.thamespathway.com
where you can see photographs of the places along walk as well as read this journal of the walk.

Finally thanks to family and friends for their encouragement and support.

Printed in Great Britain
by Amazon